Dominique Audrerie

Discovering
Périgord

Translated by Angela Moyon

ÉDITIONS SUD OUEST

Périgord is a quiet little corner of countryside where people enjoy a measured, secure existence. The landscape is filled with curve upon curve, in a series of undulating valleys and hills. The villages huddle round a Romanesque church, near the tiny covered market with its timber or stone pillars. Battlements, turrets or dovecotes suddenly come into view round the bend of a river, at the top of a rock or on the gently-rolling hillsides.

Guy de Larigaudie

Just off the Thenon to Montignac road stands the tiny Chapel of Saint-Rémy, near the village of Auriac-en-Périgord. It has an indefinable charm which seems to encapsulate all that the Périgord region has to offer.

OPPOSITE:
La Roque-Gageac in the light of the setting sun, considered to be the most beautiful village in France.

Périgord! 'Tis a name with a ring to it, the stuff that dreams are made of.

Man settled beside rivers and in the valleys in prehistoric times, leaving behind unique reminders of the lifestyles and beliefs of the day. Countless castles, churches, old villages, typical Périgord hamlets and fortified hilltop towns follow each other in beauty spots that change with the passing seasons.

The slow progress of time has shaped the area, bringing to it a human dimension.

A trip through Périgord is an exciting adventure which not only takes time but also requires a great capacity for observation, because this is no homogeneous region. Instead, it has a wide variety of landscapes running one into the other, almost without transition. Now, at the end of a long and eventful history that has brought it its unity, it has all the characteristics of an age-old region seeking the type of future that befits an area with such an outstanding heritage.

The *département* of Dordogne covered almost the whole of Périgord when it came into being in 1790. It stretches over an area of 9,225 sq. km, making it one of the largest *départements* in France, but it has a very low population density. The *département* gets its name from the R. Dordogne that flows through its southern part from east to west.

For generations, the relative distance from large towns ensured that the region remained fairly isolated. This is why its beauty spots and buildings have been preserved for so long, and why the sometimes doubtful additions of modern civilisation have been limited to the urban areas.

A land of contrast

Périgord is first and foremost a transitional area, with very differing landscapes that form a corresponding number of tiny, highly-individual regions.

The powerful cliffs round Sarlat are reminiscent of scenery in the Quercy while the rounded hills near Ribérac are a foretaste of the nearby Charentes. To the north, the countryside resembles the adjacent Limousin, and in the Bergerac area Périgord opens out into the plains of Aquitaine.

In geological terms, the Périgord landscape was formed over a fairly brief period, acquiring an appearance that varied according to the type of soil and tectonic movements.

Anybody travelling from north to south or east to west will see the high plateaux and green valleys of Brantôme and Tourtoirac, the arid plateaux of Thenon and Sorges where Jurassic limestone predominates and the main features are dry valleys and stone-covered hillsides, the light-coloured slopes round Ribérac with their characteristic

The cliffs at Les Eyzies by the Vézère river are a place of outstanding natural beauty that has been inhabited by man for thousands of years.

OPPOSITE: Visitors tour the Rouffignac Cave, also known as "the Cave of One Hundred Mammoths", by small-gauge railway. This picture shows the so-called "mammoth of discovery".

chalky limestone, the wooded slopes and alluvial plains near Sarlat, the dense forests of the Double and Landais areas where the soil is a mixture of sand and clay, and finally the elegantly-formed hills near Bergerac.

It is arguably, though, Central Périgord that forms the most typical link between all these areas. The Middle Isle Valley is a veritable corridor where trade and industry have flourished. This is the site of Périgord's main town, Périgueux, which has been located in a meander of the river for centuries.

The rivers that have cut deep into the Périgord landscape have served to connect very differing areas that nevertheless all belong to a single region. In the Upper Isle Valley, on the borders with the Limousin, the river flows down towards Central Périgord and widens out, further west, as it heads for Bergerac. The R. Manoire turns towards Périgueux, with the Brive and Terrasson Basins.

Further north, the R. Dronne serves a similar purpose, crossing countless small towns and villages before flowing into the R. Isle. Only the Tardoire and Bandiat curve north-westwards, to flow towards Charentes. In the south of

Périgord, the Vézère and Dordogne wend their way down from the Massif Central to the Sarlat and Bergerac areas in a series of brilliantly-lit meanders.

At the dawn of humanity

Périgord is famous for its many prehistoric sites, its cave paintings and for the outstanding importance of the prehistoric remains found by chance or as a result of organised digs.

The sheer cliffs lining the banks of the Dordogne, Vézère, Céou and Beunes or, further north, the Dronne, are pitted with natural shelters and caves which have been used by man for more than 400,000 years. Man settled in these areas because they provided a shelter for living in, water, well-stocked rivers, a game-filled hinterland but, more importantly still, rich flint seams providing the vital raw materials for the rudimentary arms or tools required for his survival. The conjunction of all these factors in a natural environment that was climatically favourable to human life all led our distant ancestors to choose this area for their settlements.

It is noticeable that the cave dwellings have been used until modern times, sometimes with alterations or additions dating from the mediaeval period or later centuries. This has given a perennial character to the history of man's presence here.

Many of the caves open to the public give an excellent picture of just how much they had to offer, especially in the area around Les Eyzies in places such as Font-de-Gaume and Combarelles (caves), or Cap Blanc and Pataud (rock shelters). Although the cave in Lascaux had to be closed to visitors in order to ensure its preservation, the accurately-copied Lascaux II provides an opportunity to see just what the decorative features in the real cave were like.

Museums in Périgueux, Brantôme and, especially, Les Eyzies, boast quite outstanding collections. Another place of interest is Le Thot, where people with no previous knowledge of the subject have a chance to learn something about prehistory.

The major sites, the ones which gave their names to various industries, are all to be found in the Les Eyzies area e.g. La Micoque (Micoquian era), Le Moustier (Mousterian), La Madeleine (Magdalanian), and, of course, the Perigordian Era.

Yet prehistory did not come to a halt with the end of the Palaeolithic Age. Périgord also has major remains dating from the Late Stone Age and the Bronze or Iron Ages. There are also large numbers of megaliths such as the passage grave in Nojals-et-Clottes and the dolmens in Brantôme or Point-du-Jour in Vergt-de-Biron, but many of them are unspectacular and in a poor state of repair.

Our ancestors, the Gauls

Périgord was the homeland of the Petrocorii, the land of the four clans that habitually gathered in a meander of the R. Isle (perhaps in Vesuna ?) near the spot where Périgueux stands today. The merger of these clans led to the creation of the nation of the Petrocorii which had its own coinage and its own territory, corresponding more or less to the area covered by the *département* today.

The old port of Limeuil, at the confluence of the rivers Vézère and Dordogne, stands on the cliff overlooked by its church.

Little material proof of their presence has survived but place-names are indicative of their settlement pattern. They include suffixes in -euil, e.g. Mareuil (literally "the great clearing") or Limeuil ("the elm clearing"), frontier-terms such as Eygurande or La Goirandie, and names such as Lanquais or La Bessède.

Few traces of housing have been uncovered to date, probably because of the fragile nature of these constructions and the continued use of the same spots over successive centuries. Digs have, though, turned up flints and pottery.

During the Roman Conquest, the Petrocorii were ordered to send five thousand men to assist Vercingetorix who was besieged in Alesia.

When, in 16 B.C., Caesar Augustus set up the province of Aquitaine, the Petrocorii's territory became one of the twenty-one administrative districts in the province. It retained its official name and its main town took the Gallic name of Vesuna, but a new lifestyle had come to the fore, with rules and architecture imported from Rome.

Vesuna was one of the busiest cities in Roman Gaul. It had a huge amphitheatre, a temple of which only the central tower remains, and a forum consisting of two large squares separated by a basilica. Large Roman baths received their water supply from several aqueducts. The city was connected to other large towns in the neighbouring area by a new network of roads. The main highways and many of the smaller roads have lasted to this day and have served as the basis for the main routes through Périgord.

Fairly large farms known as villas were built, mainly in the valleys. Numerous remains have been uncovered, in particular in Chamiers and Montcaret, and many of the place names (ending in -ac, -an, -as, or -at) serve as reminders of erstwhile Gallo-Roman settlements.

The end of Pax Romana

The invasions not only brought with them destruction and pillaging; they also resulted in profound social changes. Vesuna was obliged, at the end of the 3rd Century, to build a defensive town wall. To do so, it re-used stones taken from public buildings that had been the town's pride and joy in earlier times. Thereafter, the walled town covered an area of no more than 5.5 hectares, i.e. one-tenth of its area during the Early Empire.

FROM TOP TO BOTTOM
This cave under St. Front Cathedral was discovered in the 19th Century.

The Gothic-style cloisters in Périgueux cathedral have remained intact.

Boschaud Abbey, recently restored by young volunteers, is one of four Cistercian abbeys in Périgord.

The church in Sergeac is a Romanesque building whose upper storey was used as a defence chamber times of conflict.

OPPOSITE: The Vesuna Tower remains an outstanding reminder of the erstwhile splendour of the Gallo-Roman town.

Périgord then passed from the Visigoths to the Franks. After the 7th Century, its destiny was linked to that of independent Aquitaine. The campaigns instigated by Pippin the Short in his attempt to reconquer the province led to widespread destruction and misery in 763 A.D. and 768 A.D.

It was in 778 A.D. that the County of Périgord was first mentioned, when Charlemagne designated Widbode as Count.

The 9th Century was marked by the ravages of the Viking invasions. The Normans sailed up the rivers, attacking Périgueux, Paunat and Saint-Cyprien as they went.

It was, though, the Church which found itself required to safeguard the area's cultural heritage. After the arrival of St. Front in the early centuries of the Christian era, and the subsequent evangelisation of Périgord, the area became popular with numerous saint-hermits, many of whom founded villages or abbeys, among them Saint-Astier, Saint-Amand-de-Coly, Saint-Avit-Sénieur, and Terrasson (literally "land of St. Sour").

A few of the large abbeys enjoyed enormous influence e.g. Saint-Front, Brantôme, Paunat and Saint-Sauveur in Sarlat, and they attracted large crowds of pilgrims.

The Bishops played an active role in defending the area, joining the new castle-owners who built fortresses designed to defend one particular part of the territory. It was these stretches of land that gradually became the rural estates.

In the Dark Ages, the population was scattered and forest covered nearly the entire region.

At the centre of seemingly endless conflict
The divorce of Eleanor of Aquitaine and King Louis VII and Eleanor's subsequent remarriage in 1152 to Henry Plantagenet led to one of the longest wars in history, bet-

St. Stephen's Church (Saint-Étienne de la Cité), in Périgueux, is a beautiful Romanesque church. It was Périgueux's Cathedral until 1669.

ween the French monarchy and the Plantagenets. Périgord, which was still part of the Duchy of Aquitaine, was at the epicentre of the conflict and the Dordogne Valley around Bergerac was the scene of some of the bitterest fighting. Castles were built on both sides of a border that was continually being changed and resited. Fortresses such as Beynac, Castelnaud, Badefols and Montfort were captured and recaptured.

At the same time, an enormous upsurge in religious faith led to the founding of new abbeys e.g. Dalon, Cadouin, Peyrouse, and Boschaud. The churches, too, were altered and extended (St. Stephen's and St. Front's in Périgueux). The Mendicant Orders, Friars Minor and Friars Preachers, founded communities in urban centres while the Knights Templar and the Knights Hospitaller of St. John of Jerusalem set up commanderies in Les Andrivaux, Comberanche, Condat-sur-Vézère and Sergeac.

The villages grew in size and strengthened their communal rights, while rural life enjoyed a period of development. One particular feature of this period was the building of the bastides, new fortified hilltop towns some of which (Villefranche, Eymet, or Domme) were built by the French

while others (Monpazier, Lalinde and Molière) were built by the English. They not only people to adopt a more sedentary lifestyle and constituted one of the factors in economic expansion; they were also part of a system of defence.

In the 14th and 15th Centuries, Périgord was still the subject of discord between the Kings of France and England. The Treaty of Brétigny, signed in 1360, brought the whole of Périgord under English rule but, at the behest of Charles V, the Count of Périgord revolted, with many of the local barons. A number of towns were besieged. Duguesclin stayed in Périgueux for several months. Yet some of the lords remained loyal to the English crown.

At the same time, the town of Périgueux was at loggerheads with Count Archambaud V of Périgord and his heirs and it was this dispute which was to lead, in the end, to the banishment of his successors.

It was not until 1453 that Charles VII, through a campaign led by the monarch himself, succeeded in winning a number of decisive victories, in particular the Siege of Castillon. Moreover the English General, Talbot, was killed.

The local population had again suffered badly as a result of all the tension and discord. In many places, it had been

Biron Castle.

The Hôtel de la Joubertie in Périgueux.

decimated by epidemics and famine. Yet Périgord, thereafter united with the crown of France for all time, was to enjoy a period of revival in the 15th Century.

The Renaissance period

The economic revival was encouraged by the sovereign who was wily enough to confirm the fiscal and administrative priliveges enjoyed by the towns and monasteries and to uphold ancient customs, thereby instilling a renewed sense of confidence. However, the monarchs were also careful to strengthen their own authority over the feudal lords and the main towns. Royal agents played a vital role in this, sometimes to the detriment of the upper middle classes who had been responsible for governing the town prior to the agents' arrival. This was the case in Périgueux.

Despite the occasional ravages caused by the Black Death and recurring famines, there was a noticeably marked interest in artistic creation during this period. Literary circles in Périgueux, Bergerac or Sarlat attracted the sharp-minded and well-read intelligensia and it was this society that was to produce the 16th-century trio of Brantôme, Montaigne and La Boétie.

Churches were rebuilt and castles were altered and improved, often in line with ideas put forward by the Italian Renaissance, a style that Périgord's young noblemen had been able to see and admire during the Italian Campaign. Lanquais, Biron, Mareuil, Puyguilhem or Fénelon are particularly fine examples of this style. In the towns, superb new mansions were built. Sarlat was almost entirely redeveloped. Périgueux acquired wonderful new townhouses. And Montluc wrote, "I am a well-travelled man but I think that there is nothing to equal this region as regards wealth, commodities, and food". War, though, this time of a religious nature, was to lead to misery and tension again.

OVERLEAF, LEFT AND RIGHT: **Puyguilhem Castle.**

The château de L'Herm, where Eugène Le Roy situated the action of *Jacquou le Croquant*, his famous novel published in 1899.

The Wars of Religion

The Reformation spread into Périgord from the south, per-haps as a result of Henri of Navarre's holding court in Nérac. The new ideas were to spread along the banks of the R. Dordogne and on up to Périgueux, attracting mainly urban populations and the higher echelons of the aristocracy.

During Lent of the year 1544, Guillaume Marentin prea-ched Calvin's ideas in Bergerac. In Périgueux, Simon Brossier, a minister from Geneva, held meetings in the Green Hat Hostelry (Hôtellerie du Chapeau Vert).

Conciliation proved impossible, and the inevitable out-come was an upsurge of violence. "A monstrous war", wrote Montaigne.

In Périgord, fighting was frequent and bloody. There were military operations, mostly in the form of skirmishes, lightning attacks, and sieges of towns, castles or churches not to mention acts of brigandry. Periods of calm were short-lived.

The greatest leaders of the warring factions i.e. Coligny, Sully, and Turenne, all fought in Périgord where the fields had been left untended. The countryside was devastated.

Even after Henri IV had recanted in 1593, Périgord's Roman Catholics continued to put up strong resistance. The Leaguers of Périgueux did not finally rally until after the sovereign's coronation in 1594 when municipal privileges had been guaranteed.

The Peasants' Revolt

The Wars of Religion had brought enormous ruin in its wake – and total desolation for those living in rural areas.

In order to lighten the burden of taxation and show their ability to take action against the difficulties they were expe-riencing, the peasants drew up lists of complaints that were circulated from village to village.

Seven to eight thousand peasants (known as "Croquants") assembled in the Abzac Forest. In 1594, the king granted the adjournment of arrears and ordered an enquiry. These mea-sures were deemed to be insufficient.

The movement spread throughout the Bergerac area and finally reached the outskirts of Périgueux. The Croquants captured Grignols, Excideuil and Château-l'Evêque.

However, the peasants were to suffer major defeats by troops under the orders of Viscount of Bourdeille, Seneschal of Périgord, in Négrondes and Saint-Antoine-d'Auberoche.

The château de L'Herm's door.

A peasant's house.

Henri IV's reaction to the troubles was liberal and the peasants agreed to put an end to the uprising.

The area was then able to set about restoring its old houses and rebuilding its churches. The land was also improved.

A return to law and order

As Anne-Marie Cocula has said in her book, it was a slow, painstaking task trying to restore law and order in Périgord.

When Henri IV died, Périgord was racked by unrest. The Protestants of Bergerac tried to reconstitute their organisation under the leadership of Duke de La Force. Bergerac was to lose its town walls as a result.

An increase in tithes and the salt tax led to further revolt by the peasantry. Périgueux' mayor, Jay d'Ataux, had to flee the town. In country districts, the peasants' revolt (known, this time, as the "Jacquerie") began to acquire leaders such as La Mothe de la Forest on the outskirts of Périgueux, Buffarot in Monpazier and Pierre Grelety in the woods around Vergt. The uprisings were to continue until the end of Louis XIII's reign.

During the Fronde revolt, Périgord supported the insurrectionists for a while, led by its turbulent noblemen. After disorder and confusion during which combattants and leaders passed from one camp to the other, the King's troops took the initiative. Sarlat and Nontron were granted letters patent in reward for their loyalty to the sovereign. Périgueux was allowed to keep its town walls but was required to pay 25,000 livres.

The Roman Catholic Church launched the Counter-Reformation and encouraged the centres of spiritual and religious life in Périgord. Chancelade Abbey played a major role in this movement, thanks to Alain de Solminihac. Brotherhoods of Penitents sprung up in many places. There were Blue, Black and White Penitents in Périgueux, and White and Blue Penitents in Sarlat, Montignac and Terrasson, all of them dressed in long tunics in which they solemnly processed through the streets of the towns. The Company of the Holy Sacrament, which came into being in Périgueux in 1640, was also instrumental in this movement designed to encourage the reconversion of those who had chosen the Protestant faith.

During the reigns of Louis XIV and his successors, though, Périgord was also famous for its forests, iron ore and vineyards. The administrative organisation of the area was

Mareuil Castle, which still has its defensive system, was the seat of one of Périgord's four baronies.

Maréchal Bugeaud.

changed. Sub-delegations were set up in Nontron, Ribérac and Thiviers but Périgord remained isolated, well away from the new centres of business. In their memoirs, successive intendents suggested on several occasions that work should be undertaken to render the rivers navigable.

The Revocation of the Edict of Nantes led many Protestants to seek refuge abroad, mainly in Holland where there was already a network of business links set up in earlier days by traders from Bergerac.

In the days before the French Revolution, a period of relative calm, Périgord had a population of slightly more than 400,000, living mainly in rural areas. The towns of Périgueux, Bergerac and Sarlat had populations of between 6,000 and 8,000. Unlike other regions, urban development remained limited.

Nevertheless, the population was too great for the resources and employment available locally and many men decided to emigrate or join the army.

In the days immediately before the French Revolution, Périgord was a region of poor land giving mediocre crops and more densely-populated areas in which farming was

more profitable, e.g. the Dordogne and Dronne Valleys. Despite this, epidemics and, in some years, famine continued to decimate the countryside.

The French Revolution

The drawing up of the complaints books gave the local people an opportunity to indicate their short-term demands and anxieties. In every area, there were complaints about the tithe and dime and about feudal rights, as well as diatribes against the cruelty of nature and agricultural calamities. There were also echoes of those who had been influential in the "Age of Enlightenment" perhaps as a result of the many freemasons in Périgord among the upper middle classes, rural aristocracy, former military men and men of the Church.

The elections to the States General were held during the meeting of the three orders on 16th March 1789 in St. Front's Cathedral, under the chairmanship of the Marquis de Verteillac, Seneschal of Périgord. At the meeting were 240 churchmen, 240 noblemen and 380 delegates from the Third Estate. The men elected as the representatives of the

Church were Laporte, parish priest in Hautefort, and Delfau, Archpriest of Daglan (he was a victim of the September 1792 massacres). The aristocracy elected the Count de la Roque de Mons and the Marquis de Foucault de Lardimalie. And the Third Estate chose Fournier Lacharmie, Loys, Gonier de Biran and Paulhiac de la Sauvetat.

The events that shook the French capital during the Revolution did not reach Périgord until later, and often not in the same form. The enthusiasm expressed at the outset gradually gave way to anxiety. The peasants began to attack local landowners and Liberty Trees were erected throughout the region.

As events gathered momentum, more fanatical men such as Roux-Fazillac and Elie Leconte arrived in the region. Then the famous Surveillance Committees were set up and the atmosphere became more than more threatening. From April 1793 onwards, the guillotine began operating on the Place de la Clautre in Périgueux. Attempts were made to introduce revolutionary cults but the constitutional church continued to be unpopular. Some forty towns and villages were renamed so that they lost any religious connotations, among them Saint-Pantaly-d'Ans which became Pantaléon-le-Bon-Vin, Saint-Jory-de-Chalais which was renamed Chaleix-la-Montagne and Saint-Apre which became Bara-sur-Dronne. Priests were hunted down and sentenced. Castles such as the one in La Force were razed to the ground; others were severely damaged.

The coup d'état in the month of Thermidor was welcomed in Périgord with an immense general sigh of relief. Yet the wars fought by the young Republic, in which the brilliant general in the northern French army, Michel Beaupuy, won fame, were to be followed by the bloody campaigns of the Napoleonic Empire. Conscription led to a noticeable decrease in the population. The forests became the haunt of insurrectionists and brigands.

Although Périgord remained in the background during this period, many of its sons have gone down in history. Jacques Maleville was Author-Secretary of the committee responsible for drawing up the Civil Code. Lamarque, Pierre Maine de Biran, François Fournier-Sarlovèze and Daumesnil all held high office in the government or the army. First among the many, though, was Charles Maurice de Talleyrand-Périgord, a man who succeeded in carving out a place for himself in many different regimes, playing a role in the Revolution, the Empire and the restoration of the monarchy.

Daumesnil.

Lardimaldie had large vineyards before the the disastrous phylloxera epidemic in the latter years of the 19th and early years of the 20th Century.

Montaigne Castle had to be entirely rebuilt following a fire in 1885.

The iron foundry in Savignac-Lédrier lying beneath the windows of the owner's castle, has undergone a major renovation programme led by the Dordogne county council.

At La Durantie, Maréchal Bugeaud remained on his land and was able to take part in the great agricultural revival by introducing new crops and farming techniques.

Famous men to the fore

Throughout the following years, tradition and new ideas came into conflict, creating rival groups or parties within Périgord. The French Revolution brought Périgord a new form of administrative organisation and enormous changes as regards the ownership of property, much of which fell to the classes who had newly acquired wealth. This led people to say that the 19th Century was the time of famous men in Périgord.

The most famous of them all was Maréchal Thomas-Robert Bugeaud de la Piconnerie. He was the owner of La Durantie Castle and he did his best to modernise his estate by introducing more modern crop-growing and farming techniques. He was elected member of parliament but succeeded in retaining his direct, plain way of speaking despite criticism from his opponents.

Pierre Magne, who was born into a family of "serge-makers" in the Barris District of Périgueux, was member of parliament on several occasions throughout the July Monarchy and, during the Empire, he was appointed Minister of State. In his castle in Montaigne, which had been renovated, he paid particular attention to the progress achieved by his tenant farmers.

These great landowners played an active part in the revival of farming. They farmed part of their lands directly but the remainder, in fact the greater part of their estates, was rented out to tenants. This system of farming was to continue until the present century.

New land was cleared and cultivated. The population had increased considerably, and exceeded 400,000. Agricultural shows were set up, with prizes and rewards being given every year.

The 19th century was also a period of reconstruction and economic expansion, thanks to the building of the railway from 1853 onwards and the opening of huge railway repair workshops in Périgueux by the Compagnie d'Orléans.

Towns underwent a rapid population explosion. New districts were built in Bergerac, Ribérac, Nontron and, more particularly, Périgueux around the railway repair yards (Saint-Martin, Toulon and Saint-Georges Districts).

This expansion, however, was to slow down both as a result of the deep social changes that occurred in the early years of the 20th Century and because of the relative isolation of Périgord, which we have already mentioned. Because of it, Périgord never really had any industrial development.

The decline of an economic system

Because Périgord was the setting for a number of major events that occurred over a relatively short space of time, people tended to pay little attention to a rural economy that continued to exist in more or less the same form until very recent times.

First of all, it should be remembered that, from time immemorial, Périgord has always been an area of forest and woodland, and this feature set its stamp firmly on the landscape. The rural communities, or at least the more dynamic ones, had to undertake clearance in order to extend the arable land and, by doing so, they pushed back the limits of the woodland. Yet as the population began to leave the area as a result of crisis or economic problems, the forest reclaimed the land it had lost for a few years and wiped out all traces of farming.

It was the forests, and the presence of numerous, smooth-flowing rivers, that led to the setting up of ironworks in the Sarlat, Thiviers, Javerlhac and, more particularly, Nontron areas. This "proto-industry" required an abundant, but seasonal, labour force and this it found in the worker-peasants. Foundry owners were powerful people and they had to meet the many orders that were placed from outside the locality, one of their main customers being the Army which ordered the manufacture of cannons and shot. Despite this, the ironworks were unable or unwilling to adapt to changes and they had already entered a period of marked decline by the end of the 18th Century.

The iron foundries in Savignac-Lédrier.

Another business that made extensive use of local timber was glass-making, an activity centred mainly on the Double area.

The many paper mills, especially in the Couze Valley where major remains can still be seen today, made Périgord famous far and wide but they were unable to withstand competition from their rivals in the Angoulême area.

And last but not least, the potteries in Bergerac, Montpeyroux and Thiviers, which produced highly original work, remained in activity for many years, some of them until fairly recently. There again, though, the geographical location of Périgord and a certain lack of dynamism resulted in a failure to seek new outlets and products and a level of investment that proved insufficient to meet needs.

One of the main features of agriculture in Périgord, and one that also left its mark on the landscape, was wine-growing. It provided the inhabitants of rural areas with a regular source of income and a degree of prosperity. The vineyards stretched over a fairly large area and the activity was predominate in certain sectors where it has since died out altogether e.g. Ribérac, Thiviers, Savignac-les-Eglises, Sorges, Corgnac, Excideuil, Terrasson and, in Southern Périgord, Domme, Groléjac, Daglan, and the Céou Valley. Wine-growing was an expanding industry in pre-Revolutionary France and it continued to develop in the 19th Century, but it was to fall victim to the disastrous phylloxera epidemic in the latter years of the 19th and early years of the 20th Century. Only the Bergerac region succeeded in replanting vines and again producing a wine with a reputation for excellence. In the remainder of the region, the erstwhile vineyards became overgrown again, especially on the hillsides, giving the scenery the appearance it has today.

Overleaf: St. Front's Cathedral by night.

The Vesuna Tower, in Périgueux, was once the cella of a temple dedicated to the town's patron goddess, Vesuna.

OPPOSITE:
This taurobolistic autel was discovered in 1906 by the archeologist Charles Durand, between the Norman Gate and the Barrière Castle. It is dedicated to Cybèle.

Sightseeing in Périgord

Having finished our journey through time, we shall now take to the road and set out in search of the marks left on the countryside by successive generations over the centuries, a delicate and fragile development that is worth discovering and deserves our respect.

Périgueux, capital of Périgord

At the foot of the Ecorneboeuf Hills in a meander of the R.Isle lies **Périgueux** which has had an eventful history over the centuries, as witnessed by the many historic buildings in the town.

The most outstanding reminder of the splendour of the Gallo-Roman town is the Vesuna Tower. It was once the cella of a temple dedicated to the town's patron goddess, Vesuna. The tower has small bonding and is wide open on one side, apparently, or so the legend of St. Front would have it, as a result of the saint's action in driving out a demon. Major archaeological digs have made it possible to locate the exact site of the peribolos in the temple, the galleries and the peristyle. The bonding was concealed behind marble plaques added onto the wall as facing. Numerous freestones, many of them decorated, were re-used when the town walls were built in the 3rd Century. The route taken by the railway line destroyed many remains because it cut right through the middle of the Gallo-Roman town.

Behind the tower is the Bouquets Villa with extensive substructures.

The remains of the arena are in a very poor state of repair. In its day, this was a vast amphitheatre 153 metres long from north to south, seating 20,000 spectators. The building was used as support for the town wall and, more importantly, as a source of building stone when the neighbouring houses were built, among them La Rolphie Castle erected over the arena for the Counts of Périgord. It was demolished by the people of Périgord in the late 14th Century on the orders of the king.

The 3rd-century town wall can still be seen in places, and is most visible from the railway. It was built in haste and the bases of the columns and carved niches are easy to pick out. It included four gates, two of which still exist today. The area around the Norman Gate has just been cleared; it stands near the entrance to the new Jay de Beaufort High

Barrière Castle, constructed over the town walls, bears the name of the family who built it.

School. The Mars Gate has been integrated into a private block of flats.

Barrière Castle gets its name from the family who commissioned its building in the 12th Century. It backs onto the town walls and consists of a rectangular main building flanked by a keep. The bay windows with stone transoms, richly decorated door and staircase turret date from the 15th Century. Opposite the castle are narrow streets lined with houses incorporating remains from days long gone. They lead to St. Stephen's Church (église Saint-Etienne).

St. Stephen's Church was Périgueux' cathedral until 1669. It was partly destroyed by the Protestants who also damaged the Bishop's Palace. It used to have four spans that were topped by four domes with lines of pendentives and preceded by a square belltower. Of the two remaining domes, the one above the chancel was restored in 1640. The dome above the nave, which is lower, is older and totally devoid of decoration. The chancel has a flat chevet and is austerely decorated with tall, rounded arches with three lights on each side. On the north wall, note the superb 17th-century reredos and the pulpit opposite it.

Near the church is St. John's Chapel, all that remains of the erstwhile Bishop's Palace. Building began on the chapel in 1511. It has ribbed arching with liernes and tiercerons forming a layout reminiscent of a quatrefoil.

If we leave the walled town and cross the Place Francheville, we will be heading for the Puy-Saint-Front district beneath the unusual outline of the cathedral. It was in the shadow of the church and adjacent monastery that a second village began to grow up in the Middle Ages, a village that was more given to trade and which was, for many years, in conflict with the walled town.

The layout of St. Front's Cathedral, in the shape of a Greek Cross, is reminiscent of San Marco in Venice. The exterior is dominated by the impressive belltower and the five domes topped by bell turrets. It underwent major restoration in the 19th Century, under the leadership of the well-known architect, Abadie, and this makes any archaeological study rather difficult. Nevertheless the building is particularly impressive for the harmony of its volumes.

The belltower was built at the junction between the two churches i.e. the domed church and the "old church" to the west. The latter, on which building began late in the 10th Century, has only two spans supporting the belltower. In

The Norman Gate.

The great Baroque reredos in Saint Front's Cathedral depicts the Dormition and Assumption of the Virgin Mary.

front of the tower, the nave of this earlier church is now open to the sky.

Enormous pillars, squared off by passageways, are topped by ribbed arches that provide the support for the five domes set out in the form of a Cross. To square the circle, the building includes pendentives. The rounded apse was rebuilt on the site of a Gothic chapel. It contains a huge 17th-century reredos illustrating the Assumption of the Virgin Mary. The choir stalls and pulpit date from the same period.

The cloisters on the south side include two galleries dating from the 12th Century with ribbed vaulting, and two other galleries from a later period in which the ribs are almond-shaped. The chapter house opens onto the cloisters. It has ribbed arching supported on pillars. The top of the original belltower stands above the centre of the cloisters which contain a large number of carved stones taken from the building prior to its restoration.

The Puy-Saint-Front District has Renaissance mansions and old houses steeped in character. Among them is the Renaissance house on the Place du Coderc with colonettes and octagonal corner turret, the Estignard Mansion in the

Rue Limogeanne, the Gamenson House in the Rue de la Constitution, the Fayolle Residence in the Rue Barbecane, the Consul's House, and the Lambert Residence on the quay side not far from an old mill perched on a section of town wall. There is also the Abzac de Ladouze Residence and the Sallegourde House in the Rue Aubergerie. Keeping an amicably watchful eye on the community is the Mataguerre Tower, the only surviving one of the 28 towers that once fortified the walls round Puy-Saint-Front.

From the Rue des Prés, on the other side of the River Isle, a beautiful view of the Cathedral.

OPPOSITE:
In the Church of St. Stephen's in the City (Saint-Etienne de la Cité) in Périgueux, only two of the four aligned domes of the roof have survived. The church suffered badly during the Wars of Religion, when it was a cathedral.

The Mataguerre Tower is the only surviving one of the 28 towers that once fortified the walls round Puy-Saint-Front.

The outskirts of Périgueux

If you take the old Paris road, your eye will inevitably be drawn by Septfonds House, which can be seen through the trees. This is an elegant late 18th-century building designed by the architect Victor Louis.

In a clearing in the Lanmary Forest, within the boundaries of **Trélissac**, is the 15th-century Caussade Castle which is really a small fortress. It is surrounded by polygonal walls with machicolations. The gateway is enclosed in a massive tower that once contained the drawbridge. The main building backs onto the outer walls and one of the four towers in it. It has 16th-century windows with stone transoms.

A few miles from the town of **Antonne** is Les Bories. It has a rectangular central section flanked by round towers with machicolations to the north-east and north-west. To one side of the façade overlooking the entrance is a square tower containing a staircase consisting of straight flights of steps at the end of a small room on each floor. In the latter years of last century, the house became the property of the Count of Paris.

In **Bassillac** on the edge of the airport is the Château de Rognac. The windows overlooking the river have the rather unexpected addition of balconies. A circular tower with machicolations juts out like a spur, breaking the current in the river. A 17th-century mill stands next to the house.

On the edge of the RN 89 road not far from the **Boulazac** industrial estate is Lieu-Dieu, a country house that underwent widescale restoration last century. It gets its name ("place of God") from an episode during the Wars of Religion when the Holy Sacrament was brought here for safe keeping.

Bourdeilles has two castles, one mediaeval with an awe-inspiring octagonal keep, and the other dating from the Renaissance period and built within the feudal walls.

Chancelade Abbey on the outskirts of Périgueux still has some of the abbey buildings. Its abbot was the blessed Alain de Solminihac, a regular canon of the Augustinian Order.

Chancelade Abbey

Building work began on the minster in 1129. Although the base of the walls is Romanesque, the stonework was repaired and renovated from window height upwards in the 16th Century. The church consists of a nave with five spans and ribbed vaulting, a transept and a two-span chancel. The transept crossing is topped by a dome with pendentives. The chevet is flat. The West Front is on a slightly lower level and has a porch with a pointed, or Gothic, arch. On the upper level, on a string-course supported by modillions is arcading running down onto turned colonettes. The square belltower with upper storeys stands above the transept crossing.

The minster contains some fine fittings including a number of reredos and choirstalls and a collection of religious artwork housed in one of the sacristies.

The monastery buildings stand in front and to the north of the church. Bourdeille House, now the vicarage, is flanked by two towers. The abbot's lodgings, set slightly apart from the other buildings, dates from the 16th Century. It consists of two corner pavilions and a gallery that was once an orange grove.

La Rolphie in **Coulounieix** is an interesting Renaissance building. The main section is preceded by a forepart that no longer has its original columns. Above it are corbelled corner turrets and a gallery that runs partway along the façade. It is decorated with superb carvings and it is an immense pity that it has been left to fall into such disrepair.

There are many other country houses and mansions to visit on the outskirts of Périgueux, but it is time to continue on our way.

En route for Upper Périgord

A drive through the districts mushrooming on the outskirts of Périgueux and extending apparently unceasingly along the main roads will take us in the direction of Upper Périgord.

First of all, though, let us stop and take a look at **Chancelade**. Nestling at the foot of low hills overlooking the Beauronne river, Chancelade has an abbey built for Austin canons.

Near the minster is the former parish church, now St. John's Chapel. The West Front was built in the purest of Romanesque styles and includes a porch with four curves and

The Renaissance castle of Bourdeilles is richly furnished.

slightly pointed arching. There is a semi-circular bay above a projecting cornice. The gable end is decorated with a carving of the Paschal Lamb. The apse is semi-circular. The nave has two spans with ribbed barrel vaulting.

A few miles further on is **Merlande** Priory, in a clearing in the midst of the woods. There is now only one monastery building left standing, but it has been carefully restored. The church has a two-span nave, one roofed with ribbed barrel vaulting and the other topped by a dome. The entrance to the chancel is a small semi-circular door. Around the chancel is arcading supported by colonettes with superb capitals. Defensive chambers were built into the upper storey and the north-east corner of the building includes fortifications.

From Bourdeilles to Brantôme

The Dronne wends its way lazily past cliffs topped by Bourdeilles Castle. Its massive outline dominates the village and the mill once owned by the lord of the manor standing on a small island shaped like the bow of a boat. A Gothic bridge with a projecting pier-head juts out into the river bed.

Bourdeilles was the seat of one of the four baronies in Périgord and consists, on closer inspection, of two castles. There is a mediaeval fortress standing at the tip of the spur of rock; it still has its fortifications. The gateway, which once had a drawbridge, lies between two round towers. The main apartments are topped by a tall octagonal keep with machicolations.

The Renaissance castle was built for Jaquette de Montbron. It consists of a rectangular building with two storeys separated by string-courses and has mullioned windows. The staircase, with straight flights of steps, is housed in another building adjacent, and at right angles, to the main apartments. The castle is richly furnished and it is said that one of the bedchambers was laid out especially for Catherine of Medicis although she never stayed in the castle.

Further up the Dronne Valley, the most attractive valley in the *département* according to geographer Adolphe Joanne, the landscape is one of rocky scarp slopes that have been inhabited by man since prehistoric times.

In Brantôme, the R. Dronne flows more slowly, dividing into several branches that seem to be trying to give the town greater protection.

31

Standing proudly between cliffs and river, the impressive Brantôme Abbey is made up of a number of buildings dating from different periods. It was extensively restored during the 19th Century.

OPPOSITE:
Brantôme Abbey's belltower.

One of the caves situated behind the abbey contains a large sculpture cut into the wall depicting a scene from the Last Judgement.

Brantôme, built in the shadow of the Benedictine abbey that has been very influential over the centuries, now uses the prestigious historic building for a range of activities linked to its initial purpose.

The huge limestone cliff is dotted with countless caves that were used for religious ceremonies in the days of Antiquity. They were soon given a Christian significance by hermits attracted to this evocative spot early in the history of Christianity. The strangest sight of all, though, is undoubtedly the huge bas-relief housed in the largest of the caves. Certain archaeologists believe that it illustrates a scene from the Last Judgement, hence its name.

It was Charlemagne who had the relics of St. Sicaire brought to the monastery and crowds of pilgrims then visited it to pray. The church once had a line of domes, but they have now disappeared. In the 11th Century, the monks had a gabled belltower built, supported partly by the rock, and it is one of the most interesting towers in the region. After many ups-and-downs, restoration work was finally begun last century, under the leadership of Abadie, the architect who designed St. Front's Cathedral. He had no hesitation in removing, changing and redesigning the building in accordance

with his own views, and it was he who gave it the appearance it has today. Although it is perhaps regrettable that we no longer have the mediaeval castle built for Pierre de Mareuil between the river and the abbey, nor most of the cloisters, the abbey has nevertheless retained all its original elegance as is evident when seen from the angled bridge.

Beyond the bridge is the monks' garden with its Renaissance wayside altars, an ideal spot for meditation, following the example set by Brantôme who chronicled the period in which he lived and whose portrait can be seen on the nearby Medicis Fountain.

Nontron in Green Périgord
The road to **Nontron** crosses stretches of increasingly impenetrable forest and runs along the banks of an increasing number of rivers and streams. This is Green Périgord.

In a clearing on the edge of the road is the delicate Château de la Pouyade with its tiny 18th-century chapel set slightly to one side. Further along the road are countless other old country houses, e.g. Vieillecourt, Vaugoubert, Montcheuil and Labertie, for the Nontron area also has a large number of historic buildings that are too little known

and which are scattered across a landscape that has changed but little over the years.

The town of Nontron, which has been a sub-prefecture since the beginning of the century, is strung out along a spur of rock. The Place Paul Bert was once the site of a feudal castle and a Romanesque church. Inside the town, an 18th-century castle built over the town walls now houses a doll museum. In the lower part of the town are old half-timbered houses currently undergoing renovation. An impressive viaduct, now deserted by the railway, crosses the Bandiat Valley. Be sure not to leave Nontron without buying yourself a penknife with a boxwood handle decorated with poker-work. This is the town's best-known souvenir.

Within the boundaries of **Lussas-et-Nontronneau** are the remains of a vast Gallo-Roman villa. Not far away is the 16th-century Beauvais Castle flanked by towers with machicolations.

In **La Chapelle-Saint-Robert**, the 12th-century chapel that was once the centre of a priory is an excellent example of local churches with its square belltower decorated with arcading built above the transept crossing, its semi-circular apse, and its capitals carved in the style of the Saintonge region.

In the small town of **Javerlhac** is a 16th-century castle

that has undergone extensive alteration over the following centuries. It is reflected in the waters of the Bandiat, not far from the watermill that still contains its ancient machinery. In the 18th Century, the Marquis de Montalambert established a number of iron foundries, including the New Forge which still has its blast-furnace.

The castle in **Varaignes** was bought back by the town council in order to avoid total ruin. The finely-carved door had already been sold off to an architecture buff from across the Atlantic. Encircled by its parapet walkway, it has a superb Renaissance frontage overlooking the courtyard.

On the borders with the Limousin area

The church in **Bussière-Badil** (12th Century with 16th-century alterations) has a triple doorway, each arch supported on colonnettes with finely-carved capitals. It includes a nave and two side aisles with barrel vaulting. The transept crossing is roofed with a dome over pendentives which are, themselves, rather unusually supported by small squinches. Above is an octagonal belltower. The apse is semi-circular. The church was given a system of defence in later years. It was doubtless its geographical location which

Puyguilhem, near Villars, is a "Loire-Valley Renaissance castle lost in Périgord".

brought to it artists from the schools of Périgord, Limousin and Angoulême.

The region also has several vast lakes. **Grolhier** is of particular ecological interest; **Saint-Estèphe** has been laid out for swimming and leisure. Nearby is the Logan Stone, a block of granite balanced precariously on a rocky slab. All along the waterways are mills that once produced oil and flour.

Piégut lies in the shadow of a circular keep, all that remains of a castle built on a feudal motte and destroyed in 1199 by Richard the Lionheart.

Near **Abjat** is the Charelle Bridge, steeped in memories of the conflict that opposed the Lord of Vaucaucourt to the local peasantry who were disgusted by the noblemen's penchant for women. He lost his life in the scuffle and, for many years thereafter, Abjat was deprived of bells and fairs.

Saint-Saud-Lacoussière has the remains of La Coussière Castle, which was dismantled during the One Hundred Years War. Not far away are the ruins of Peyrouse Abbey, one of the four Cistercian abbeys in Périgord.

After crossing **Saint-Pardoux-la-Rivière** that grew up around a ford in the river and stopping to look at the

Puyguilhem

The central apartments, which have an upper storey, include mullioned windows. Above them are highly-ornate dormer windows. On the main façade is a huge round tower in one corner. In the other is a rectangular tower with quoins. The towers also include some fine dormer windows at roof level. Behind the central apartments are two projecting wings of different sizes. The decorative features are exquisite, both inside and outside the castle. The ears of corn, curled crockets, moulded string-courses, finials, spires, niches and tiny figures come as a surprise in this area of Périgord, both for their quality and for their sheer number.

remains of the Dominican monastery that was particularly active until the outbreak of the French Revolution, cross the R. Dronne by the tiny Romanesque bridge in **Quinsac**.

A "Loire-Valley Castle" in Périgord
Puyguilhem Castle within the boundaries of **Villars** is reminiscent of the wonderful residences on the banks of the R. Loire built during the early years of the Renaissance.

ABOVE:
Fire devastated La Chapelle-Faucher Castle, which stands on a clifftop overlooking the R. Cole.

OPPOSITE:
The remains of Boschaud Abbey.
The Romanesque church still has part
of the chancel and transept

A short distance away are the Villars Caves. They are full of stalactites and stalagmites and prehistoric remains have been found in them.

Do not leave Villars without visiting the remains of Boschaud Abbey. The Romanesque church still has part of the chancel and transept, both of them roofed with a dome over pendentives. Part of the cloisters have been given back their original appearance thanks to work by young volunteers.

Travelling up the Côle Valley

La Chapelle-Faucher is an impressive sight, a castle standing high on the cliff top above the R. Côle. It still has its curtain walls and its postern gate at the entrance topped by a steeply-sloping roof. The roofs of the castle were destroyed by fire in 1916 after the building was struck by lightning. This left open to the air a vast set of apartments dating from the 15th and 16th Centuries flanked by two massive circular towers on the courtyard side. In the centre is a polygonal tower containing the spiral staircase that used to run up to the various storeys. The windows and dormers, decorated with tiny figures, now open onto thin air. At the end of the courtyard is a manege next to the stables. It is said

Jumilhac Castle, with its odd-shaped high slate roofs, is perched on a spur of rock overlooking the Isle Valley.

The majestic ruins of Bruzac, on a cliff overlooking the R. Côle, consist of two castles which were owned by two joint lords.

that the castle was besieged by none other than the Black Prince.

In the village church, an 18th-century statue of the Virgin Mary keeps watch at the main door.

A short distance away are the ruins of the castle or, to be more precise, the castles of **Bruzac**, standing guard over a valley in the midst of thick vegetation. The castles used to be surrounded by one and the same wall, defended by several towers and preceded by a dry moat. They still have some fine Renaissance windows, doors and fireplaces indicating the levels of the various floors.

The small town of **Saint-Pierre-de-Côle** has an elegant Romanesque church with a rounded porch decorated with two curves set in a forepart. The interior, though, underwent extensive restoration in the 19th Century. On the banks of the R. Côle is the Lepers Chapel. On the West Front is a series of slender colonettes with "lepers' squints" from which people could attend Mass without entering the building.

Further along the shores of the meandering R. Côle is the delightful little town of **Saint-Jean-de-Côle** which boasts a number of historic buildings. The old main street is lined with half-timbered houses.

The church, originally a minster, has a fairly unusual layout. A single span in the nave extends into a central apse that was used as a chancel. To each side are radiating apsidal chapels dating from the 11th and 12th Centuries. The nave used to be roofed with a huge dome but it collapsed as a result of a structural defect. It was replaced by a timber roof. The chevet and apsidal chapels are decorated with carvings such as Daniel in the lions' den, or the creation of man.

Two sides of the 16th-century cloisters still exist. Huge, round pillars provide support for tierce-point arches. An upper gallery broken up by spiral columns used to open onto the monks' cells.

Adjacent to the abbey is La Marthonie, a manorhouse with tall walls and mullioned windows. The keep still has its original roof above the parapet walkway. One of the wings set at right angles was built in the 17th Century, over an arcaded gallery. Inside, a staircase dating from the same period leads to the upper storeys.

A few yards down the road is a hump-backed bridge reflected in the water. There is no risk of damage from cars – they are too wide to cross it.

The old abbey church in Saint-Jean-de-Côle stands right in the centre of the village. The covered market, supported by wooden posts, lies adjacent to the apse.

Thiviers and its foie gras markets

Thiviers is always a busy shopping centre between Périgueux and Limoges but on market days, the hustle and bustle reaches its climax. On days such as those, in the right season, traders or private individuals crowd round the stalls, carefully and meticulously examining the goose or duck livers. What a delight for gourmets – and those with a healthy appetite!

Near the Tourist Office is the Foie Gras, Goose and Duck Centre (maison du foie gras, de l'oie et et canard) which demonstrates the various stages in the production of one of the most famous of all Périgord's dishes.

Thiviers has two castles, each of them altered on many occasions. They are Vaucaucourt and Banceil. The church has a double-spanned nave and a chancel with ogival vaulting. The arms of the transept have barrel vaulting. The Romanesque capitals are superbly carved.

Further east lies the village of **Nantheuil**. It is a picturesque place with a castle and a fortified priory church.

From there, head back upstream to Jumilhac.

Jumilhac Castle

Jumilhac Castle is often described as "romantic". The extreme complexity of its roof gives it a highly unusual appearance. Sections shaped like candle-snuffers or bishops' mitres topped by lead finials are broken up by dormer windows with an apparently total disregard for any order. Built at the very tip of a spur of rock, it includes building techniques from various periods of history. The frontage of the main apartments dates from the 14th Century and include countless projections and undulations. Above them is a parapet walkway defended by machicolations. In the 17th Century, two wings were added on at right angles to the remainder of the building. They are completed by rectangular corner pavilions. The courtyard is closed off by a huge wall.

Inside, the most interesting room is the so-called "Spinner's Chamber" in which a fickle wife, Louise de Hautefort, was shut away by her husband, Antoine de Jumilhac. Legend has it that she spent the remainder of her life spinning wool and that the yarn ran down the walls, giving her a means of keeping in contact with her lover. It was Henri IV who gave the castle to a foundry owner named Antoine Chapelle, in gratitude for the cannons supplied by him to the monarch.

39

A region in rich in iron foundries

A region rich in iron foundries

The road to **Jumilhac-le-Grand** is particularly picturesque. It crosses the Upper Isle Valley, a deep narrow gorge lined with abandoned foundries and superb manorhouses bearing witness to the erstwhile grandeur of the foundry owners.

Lanouaille is steeped in memories of Maréchal Bugeaud who, in the castle of La Durantie, tried to introduce new farming techniques. The outbuildings near the castle are an indication of the size of the estate at that time, and his determination to rationalise his lands.

In **Vaud**, there are extensive remains of an old iron foundry which are still easy to see. There are others at numerous sites along the Auvézère Gorge, an area that proved particularly suitable for iron foundries and watermills.

It is, though, in **Savignac-Lédrier** that the most characteristic of the foundries is to be seen. It remained in operation from 1421 to 1930, producing very high-quality iron. It employed large numbers of people in the production of the iron itself and in the transport of raw materials. The blast-furnace, covered market, workers' houses and all the foundry buildings are still in place, with their machinery. The

département of Dordogne, now the owner of this site, has launched a restoration project.

The foundry owner's house dominates the remainder of the foundry buildings. It has a central section with a round tower to each side. Although the buildings are mediaeval in origin, they were altered during the Renaissance period. A superb gateway decorated with 16th-century arabesques has been preserved in the gardens.

Excideuil ans the Ans area

The small town of **Excideuil** used to lie in the shadow of a mighty castle, but all that remains of the fortress today are two 14th-century square keeps and two Renaissance buildings. The barbican at the entrance is flanked by two engaged turrets. The local council has turned the outhouses into meeting rooms.

At the top end of the town is the parish church, once the seat of a Benedictine priory. There is a superb Flamboyant Gothic doorway in the south wall.

At the confluence of the rivers Isle and Loue in a truly delightful setting stands **Coulaures**. La Cousse Castle is a fine 16th and 17th-century residence. The main section

includes elegant corner pavilions. The domed church dating from the Romanesque period has undergone extensive restoration. On the banks of the river is Notre-Dame chapel, a charming 17th-century building with a tall roof topped by a lantern turret.

The castle in **Mayac** is filled with memories of brilliant soirées that attracted all the local nobility in the years leading up to the French Revolution. It is a vast quadrilateral dating from the late 17th Century, flanked by two turrets. It was extensively altered last century.

In the Ans area, there are more old foundries, and the houses that belonged to the owners are still a fine sight. Many of the towns and villages include the name of the area in their own names e.g. **La Boissière d'Ans, Saint-Pantaly d'Ans, Sainte-Eulalie d'Ans, Grange d'Ans**.

Chourgnac, a small farming community, was the birthplace of a king, Orélie-Antoine I, King of Araucania and Patagonia. His real name was Antoine Tounens and he visited South America several times from 1860 onwards. He eventually succeeded in persuading the indigenous peoples to take him as their sovereign.

Hautefort, the king of all castles

On its rocky promontory, **Hautefort** Castle presents passing strangers with exactly the picture desired in the 17th Century by Jacques-François de Hautefort. He was assisted in his efforts by Nicolas Rambourg and, later, Jacques Maigret.

The castle stands at the top of a rise and only comes into view gradually, one section at a time, starting with the tall slate roofs, followed by the walls with their great mullioned windows and ending with the fortified gatehouse in the centre, at the end of a vast esplanade.

The entrance is on the side of the building. It has retained its defensive appearance with its crenelated barbican and wooden drawbridge.

The castle is laid out in a huge quadrilateral. On one side are the impressive apartments on several floors, stretching from east to west and flanked by powerful pavilions. Two wings set at right angles back onto the massive round towers topped with domes and lantern turrets. On the fourth side, the courtyard forms a terrace opening onto a wide expanse of surrounding countryside.

The ground floor is lit by a fine row of alternating basket and semi-circular bays. At the base of the main part of

ON PREVIOUS PAGES:
Hautefort Castle juts out from the centre of a vast amphitheatre where, according to records, a fortress belonging to the Viscounts of Limoges existed as far back as the 9th Century.

FROM TOP TO BOTTOM

There are many watermills dotted along the R. Auvézère such as this one in Pervendoux situated in the picturesque river gorge.

The wealthy farms in the Ans region are a reminder that this is a region with a rural tradition.

The Château de Rastignac was built by the Marquis of Rastignac in the early 19th Century. Based on plans drawn up by the Périgord architect Mathurin Blanchard, it bears a strange resemblance to the White House.

The Barade Forest.

the building is a delightful gallery opening onto the courtyard. On the upper floor, there are tall windows with double transoms beneath triangular pediments. The chapel is housed in the east wing.

The overall effect is one of restrained decoration yet the building as a whole has a grandiose appearance thanks to its size and its austerity.

The apartments in the interior have been tastefully furnished. Two staircases run up to the upper floor. The west stairs lead to the private apartments; to the east is the main staircase.

After the terrible fire that raged through the château in 1968, Baroness de Bastard launched a systematic restoration of the entire building in order to give the residence back its past splendour.

Hautefort was also the birthplace of Bertran de Born, the famous troubadour.

Visitors should not leave Hautefort without seeing the gardens and park and, on the outskirts of the village, the almshouse. It stands in the middle of the square used for fairs and markets and has four wings laid out in the shape of a Cross around a central dome above the chancel in the chapel.

The village of Bars in the heart of the Barade Forest has a church with wall-belfry. It calls to mind the story of Jacquou le Croquant.

Terrasson, the gateway to the Brive area

Terrasson has been built in a semi-circle on the hillside. Rows of slate roofs tumble down the slope from the church. The town grew up in the shadow of a Benedictine abbey and its name came from that of a pious hermit called St. Sour who brought Christianity to the region. The cave to which he is said to have retired is in the cliff on the western outskirts of the town.

There used to be town walls but little remains of them today. In the old town, the narrow streets are lined with Renaissance houses and mansions named after their erstwhile owners e.g. Lacoste, Marcillac, or Brossard. The church, once a minster, was built in the shape of a Cross. Despite alterations in the latter years of last century, it has retained its 15th-century Flamboyant Gothic doorway, part of which has been walled up. From the terrace, there is a view of the valley and the more recent parts of the town. An old Gothic bridge with pier-heads crosses the R. Vézère; it is for pedestrians only.

Fraysse Castle to the east of the town was built in the 18th Century over older foundations and it still has the substructures once used for its system of defence. Further south is Montmège Castle, an interesting building with architectural features from several different centuries. The windows in the front are decorated with colonettes, transomes, tracery and carved consoles.

Lavilledieu is an ancient parish that has been annexed to Terrasson. It has a 16th-century church which underwent extensive alterations during the last century. In the belltower-wall is the oldest bell in Périgord, said to date from the Carolingian era.

Condat-Le-Lardin is best-known for its large paper mill which has been producing high-quality paper for many years. Condat was also the site of a commandery of the Knights Hospitaller of St. John of Jerusalem. All that remains today is the church and a building strengthened with square towers topped by machicolations. In the neighbouring houses are turrets and decorative features taken from the commandery.

Le Lardin boasts Peyraux House, a fine mansion dating from the 17th and 18th Centuries including a 15th-century tower. It was built on a hillside.

In Condat the Cern and, beyond it, the Manoire Valleys join the Vézère Valley. The Manoire Valley takes you back to Périgueux.

The church in Saint-Armand-de-Coly was designed like a veritable fortress. It has a complete system of defence both inside and out, making it one of the of most interesting buildings in Périgord.

The church in Saint-Amand-de-Coly has a grandiose yet almost military austery. The nave slopes gradually up towards the chancel.

OPPOSITE:
In front of the West Front are two massive stone piers bearing the weight of the ribbed barrel vaulting some distance off the ground, topped by a defensive chamber that is a sort of keep.

From the main road, in **La Bachellerie**, you can see a mansion which bears a certain resemblance to the White House. Built in the early years of the 19th Century in a very pure architectural style, Rastignac House has a semi-circular peristyle at the top of a flight of stone steps. The interior suffered serious damage at the end of the Second World War.

The town hall in **Azerat** is now housed in a former castle. The tiny Gothic chapel of Our Lady of Good Hope (Notre-Dame de Bonne-Espérance) was a place of pilgrimage long ago in its history.

The road along the valley runs through old villages huddling round their church. They skirt the southern edge of the Barade Forest made famous by the novel *Jacquou le Croquant*.

The Coly Valley

Condat lies at the entrance to the wild, untamed Coly Valley whose river banks are dotted with watermills.

In **Coly**, you can see the ruins of the fortress that once belonged to the abbots from the Abbey of **Saint-Amand-de-Coly**. The Romanesque church, with its belltower-wall, has undergone extensive alterations.

The Abbey of Saint-Amand-de-Coly stands high above the tiny village huddling round the foot of its walls. The minster is the most interesting religious buiding in Périgord because it includes a system of defence that gives it a most unusual appearance.

Sited in a particularly vulnerable spot, the entire building was designed as a fortress. In front of the West Front are two massive stone piers bearing the weight of the ribbed barrel vaulting some distance off the ground, topped by a defensive chamber that is a sort of keep. Above the entrance is a row of supports which could have been used for a wooden floor. At the other end of the church, the chevet includes apsidal chapels beyond a number of steps built into the hillside.

The interior of the church is striking for its simplicity and inherent beauty. The aisle rises up to the chancel. The nave has ribbed barrel vaulting. Engaged pillars bear the four arches supporting a dome over pendentives. The raised chancel ends in a flat chevet with three windows and a round window at the top and is roofed with ribbed vaulting. A circular pavement runs rounds the building, combining with other features such as concealed staircases, hollow pillars, and passageways cut into the thickness of the walls.

Montignac, a market town by the R. Vézère, is most famous for its proximity to the Lascaux cave.

TOP:
Lascaux: one of the "Chinese horses" in the side passage.
BOTTOM:
Lascaux: a bison.

ON PREVIOUS PAGES:
After a chance discovery by children in 1940, the Lascaux cave has become the "Sixtine Chapel" of prehistory. Although the cave is closed to the public in order to ensure its preservation, a replica has been built nearby giving visitors an opportunity to see the famous cave paintings. This picture shows the "Great Bull" which was photographed in the original cave.

Half-hidden in a rural valley is La Grande Filolie, a dissymetrical mansion that consists of a 15th-century nobleman's residence and a Renaissance manorhouse set out around a courtyard that is also flanked by the outbuildings and chapel. The gatehouse is topped by a bartizan. The stepped roof was built of flat stone slabs called lauzes.

Let us now return to the Vézère Valley via **Montignac**.

The Valley of Man

The Vézère Valley is the site of several prestigious, world-famous locations bearing witness to the history of mankind since the dawn of time. Over the centuries, man has left tangible proof here of his creative genius.

Montignac boasts the most famous of all caves – Lascaux. It contains an outstanding set of cave paintings dating from the Early Magdalanian. A succession, and combination, of bison, bulls, and horses cover the walls of the great chamber and the two side passages in prehistory's own "Sistine Chapel".

Lascaux was discovered in 1940 by children out to play in the depths of the woodland. Now closed in order to ensure its preservation, a replica of the original cave never-

theless gives visitors a chance to see this piece of artistic and historical heritage.

Montignac is a peaceful little town whose world was turned upside down by the discovery of the Lascaux cave. From the bridge, there is a view of the old houses, some of them built on terraces and others, with half-timbering, stretching out along the river banks. The priory church dates from the 12th Century. Nearby is a building that calls to mind the school of Nicolas Ledoux, the famous 18th-century architect. It was in Montignac that Eugène Le Roy died. He was the author of Jacquou le Croquant and a number of other, regionally-based novels.

Losse Castle within the boundary of **Thonac** stands on a natural platform overlooking the R. Vézère. It consists of two buildings set at right angles to each other and flanked by a round tower at the outer corner. A crenelated parapet walkway runs right round the castle. In front of it is a fortified gateway with a superb roof of flat stone slabs. Built in the second half of the 16th Century, it still has the system of defence from an earlier period that blends so well into the Renaissance architecture.

A short distance away is Belcayre Castle, which is also

In Thonac, a picturesque village in Périgord Noir, there are frequent reminders of the fact that flat stone slabs were a common roofing material in this area.

Losse Castle stands on a terrace overlooking the R. Vézère. Access is by way of a fortified gate.

Belcayre Castle was built on a rock in the shape of a ship's bow.

Rouffignac church and its fine Renaissance portal is all that remains of the village, which was totally destroyed by German troops at the end of the Second World War.

set in a picturesque spot on the banks of the R. Vézère. It has a main building topped with machicolations, and a cylindrical tower.

The 12th-century Vermondie Tower on a hilltop is unusual in that it stands at an angle. Legend has it that this is because a lady who was shut up in the very top room in the tower by her husband tried her hardest to reach her lover down below.

Saint-Léon-sur-Vézère lies within a meander of the river. Beside the church are two castles. The magnificently restored church dates from the 12th Century. The domed nave opens onto a rounded apse set between two apsidal chapels. Unusual passageways known as "berrichons" conceal the front corners of the nave. During the summer season, the church is used for the Black Périgord Music Festival. Clérans Castle is a graceful 16th-century building. La Salle Manor has a fine 14th-century keep with a vast roof of stone slabs.

On Jor Hill stands Chabans Castle, a 16th and 17th-century building with two sections set at right angles to each other. The staircase is contained in a polygonal tower. Not far from the castle, there is a Tibetan community which attracts numerous followers.

The 12th-century belfry-keep towers over the village of Plazac.

The village of Saint-Léon-sur-Vézère,
situated within a meander of the R. Vézère, has a
Romanesque church that displays a great purity of style.
Each year during the summer season, it hosts
a programme of top class concerts.

From Le Moustier to Rouffignac

In **Peyzac-le-Moustier**, the major discoveries made beneath the Moustier Rock gave their name to one of the periods in the Stone Age – the Mousterian.

Opposite the small town is La Roque-Saint-Christophe, a large troglodyte fortress in the cliff face. It was occupied in prehistoric times and was used on several occasions in periods of conflict until fairly recently.

Further up the narrow Moustier Valley is the village of **Plazac**. The Romanesque church has an interesting square belltower. A wooden gallery links the church and the vicarage.

Rouffignac was burnt to the ground by the Germans in 1944. Only the church escaped the disaster. The West Front includes a Renaissance porch. Inside, there are three aisles, each with two spans. The ribbed vaulting is supported on elegant engaged columns decorated with spiral moulding.

Further north is L'Herm Castle, now in ruins. The main section is flanked by two round towers to one side and an octagonal turret containing the staircase to the other. Superb fireplaces dating, like the castle, from the 15th Century, cling onto the walls above empty space.

The Cro-de-Granville cave in the middle of the forest contains a large number of paintings and engravings from the Magdalanian Era and this has earned it the nickname of "the cave with the hundred mammoths". Visitors are taken on a tour by a narrow-gauge railway.

Back towards the R. Vézère, the road again runs through the Barade Forest, the subject of countless stories and legends that used to be told in local farmhouses as people sat round the fire in the evenings.

In **Tursac**, the R. Vézère gracefully turns this way and that. The small town is centred on its fortified Romanesque church. On the other side of the river is La Madeleine which has a major prehistoric site. Above the site is a troglodyte village built in later periods. Right at the top are the ruins of the feudal Petit-Marzac Castle.

Marzac Castle itself stands high above the valley. Built in the 15th and 16th Centuries, it has a rectangular main section with two round towers to one side and a square tower to the other. There are battlements right round the castle. In front of the main courtyard is a machicolated curtain wall against which are the spans of what might be called cloisters. The dovecot in the middle of the park has a strange rounded roof.

The cliffs at Les Eyzies are filled with rock shelters and prehistoric sites.

The Cro Magnon man carved by the sculptor Dardé is in fact a Neanderthal man. He stands guard over the town of Les Eyzies from the terrace of the National Prehistory Museum.

OPPOSITE:
Eyrignac Manor, to the north-east of Sarlat, has magnificent gardens which are open to the public.

The National Prehistory Museum in Les Eyzies
The National Prehistory Museum, which is currently undergoing extension, has some of the largest collections anywhere in the world. It is housed in what remains of the castle built in the 12th Century on a platform of rock halfway up the cliff. It was altered in the 16th Century and again for the purposes of the museum.

Les Eyzies, a major centre of prehistory
Les Eyzies was born, one might say, in 1863, when the first prehistoric remains came to light. The small town at the confluence of the Vézère and Beunes Valleys stretches out along each side of the road, below cliffs that are filled with rock shelters and prehistoric sites.

The greatest experts in the field of prehistory have all come to Les Eyzies, among them Lartet, Christy and Vibray, the earliest specialists, Peyrony, Father Breuil and many, many more.

La Mouthe Cave contains the first indications of prehistoric civilisation ever discovered. Cro-Magnon Man, and the Micoquian and Tayacian industries all owe their names to small hamlets in this region.

Among the many rock shelters and caves are Les Combarelles and Font-de-Gaume, both of which are State-owned and open to the public, Laugerie-Haute and Laugerie-Basse, l'Oreille d'Enfer, la Croze, la Calévie, and the Abri du Poisson ("Fish Shelter"). The Pataud shelter contains an informative explanation of the layers of earth, rock etc. as they appear during archaeological digs. Le Grand Roc has some wonderful stalactites and stalagmites.

In fact, within the town's boundary, nearly every spot has Paleolithic sites of enormous interest. Because of this, Les Eyzies has been nicknamed "the Capital of Prehistory".

Les Eyzies used to be dependent on **Tayac**, a small village huddled round its church, near the station. The church dates from the 12th Century. It was fortified and, because of this, has two crenelated defensive belltowers, one on the West Front, the other on the flat chevet. The side windows are like slit windows. The porch is topped by a slightly pointed arch with five coves decorated with a torus.

Manaurie boasts the large La Micoque site. Saint-Criq has several prehistoric sites and a cave with engravings in it, the so-called "Wizard's Cave". The site at Le Pech-Saint-Sourd is topped by a cliff fort.

The castle in **Campagne** was bequeathed to the government. It consists of two buildings set at right angles to each other, one of them ending in a square pavilion, the other in a square tower. There are two round towers adjacent to the north wall. The building, which has a tall slate roof, underwent major alteration in the 19th Century. The forest next to the castle formed a sort of extension to the park; it contains prehistoric sites and cave dwellings.

FROM TOP TO BOTTOM

The elegant castle in Campagne has undergone alteration on several occasions over the centuries and is now State-owned.

The Cap Blanc Rock Shelter has an outstanding carved frieze in high-relief dating from the Palaeolithic Era.

The huts in Le Breuilh are one of the most interesting examples of the dry stone huts that are such a common feature of the landscape in Périgord.

OPPOSITE :
The romantic ruins of Commarque Castle opposite Laussel above a prehistoric site on the edge of the Beune Valley.

The Beune Valley

The Beune Valley wends its way lazily between sheer cliffs. Numerous prehistoric sites have been discovered at the foot of the walls of rock. Halfway up the cliffs are cave dwellings, some of them still occupied until recent times.

In **Sireuil**, a short distance from the town, is Commarque Castle, high above the valley floor. It has a vast fortified outer wall that used to surround the hillfort. The castle itself consists of two adjacent keeps, one dating from the 12th Century and the other from the 14th. Inside are small rooms. A 15th-century building closes off the end of the courtyard. Although the castle lies in ruins, it has been shored up in recent years.

The castle stands above a collection of cave dwellings that form a veritable village within the cliff. A decorated cave has been found at the foot of the castle and its outbuildings.

The castle is a centre for the study of castles and operates in conjunction with the permanent environmental study centre in Sireuil.

Opposite Commarque stands Laussel Castle built in the 15th and 17th Centuries but with major 19th-century restorations. The main apartments are flanked by towers with crenelations and machicolations. The roof is made of superb stone slabs. A short distance from the castle, but on the

Near the church with its stone-slabbed roof stands Saint-Geniès Castle, which has been remarkably well restored.

same bank of the R. Beune within the boundary of **Marquay**, is the Cap Blanc Rock Shelter, which has an outstanding carved frieze in high-relief dating from the Palaeolithic Era. In the cave at La Grèze not far from the shelter, there is a carving of a bison. It was in the shelter in Laussel that the superb statuette of "Venus with a Horn" was discovered.

After a quick glimpse of the hilltop village of **Tamniès**, it is time to take the Sarlat road, but be sure to leave enough time for a short detour to Saint-Geniès.

Saint-Geniès is outstanding for the stone-slabbed roofs on each of the buildings. The Romanesque church has a bell-tower-cum-porch that was fortified in the 16th Century. All that remains of the mediaeval castle is a Romanesque keep, lying in ruins. Another castle adjacent to the church dates from the 16th Century, but it underwent extensive alterations last century. Le Cheylard Chapel was built on a rise in the Gothic style. It contains a number of frescoes that are particularly interesting.

The superb "Venus with a horn" was discovered in Laussel. It belongs now to the Aquitaine Museum in Bordeaux.

OPPOSITE:

Laussel Castle.

The rooftops of Sarlat and the belltower of Saint Mary's former parish church.

Sarlat in Black Périgord

Sarlat is one of the towns that has been most successful in preserving its ancient heritage. Situated in a dip and surrounded by hills on all sides, the town has a small river flowing through it, the Cuze, which is only visible in places.

Sarlat existed in Gallo-Roman times. Pippin the Short is said to have set up a monastery here in the 9th Century. Later, Charlemagne entrusted the body of St. Sacerdos, Bishop of Limoges, to the Benedictines. Years after that, the abbey became a daughter-house of Cluny. A total of eighty-five churches depended on the community whose mother-house was the monastery here. St. Bernard stopped in Sarlat on his return from the Albigensian Crusade and performed the miracle of the loaves that cured the locals of the Black Death. In memory of his action, the population erected the St. Bernard Tower, better known as the Lantern of the Deceased. In the early 13th Century, the town attempted to shake off the links binding it to the abbey and its abbot, and, in 1223, it set itself up as a borough. It was granted a franchise charter in 1298. At that time, it had a population of six thousand.

Sarlat became the seat of a bishopric in 1317 and it remained so until the outbreak of the French Revolution. As a fervent supporter of royalty, Sarlat suffered badly during the One Hundred Years' War. It received a visit from the Constable, Du Guesclin, in 1370. The Wars of Religion also left their mark on the area but, safe behind its ramparts, the town withstood attack. Thereafter, it entered a more peaceful period, indeed life was almost too quiet and Sarlat, set well away from the main road network, was denied any real expansion. This is no doubt the main reason for its state of preservation.

In the 19th Century, a modern street suddenly cut the town in half. Its real name is the rue de la République but it is still known as the "Traverse". A stroll through the streets of the town is a source of constant surprise. Houses with character and mansions stand side by side in apparent disorder. The Middle Ages and Renaissance periods have left a number of superb buildings and, over the past thirty years, they have benefitted from systematic restoration under the terms of a conservation project that was the first of its kind in France.

In the summer, huge crowds of tourists flock through the streets, astonished at all the architectural gems.

From top to bottom

Sarlat. The former Bishop's Palace.

Sarlat. This gate, rue de la Salamandre, opens to the Hôtel de Grézel's tower.

The town hall is an elegant 16th and 17th-century building.

The writer Etienne de La Boétie was born in Sarlat. He is mostly well-known because he was Montaigne's best friend.

All that remains of the old town walls, apart from a few stretches of masonry, is the Executioner's Tower (tour du Bourreau) and the Pech Cross Tower (tour de la Croix du Pech).

Bishop Armand de Genteuil destroyed almost all the original minster in the 16th Century when he was engaged in the building of the cathedral, with the exception of the walls that linked the chevet to the apsidal chapels and the impressive belltower adjacent to the West Front. The entrance is a Classical doorway. Above it, slender blind arcading forming a triple arch marks out the first storey; the second storey has four slightly pointed semi-circular bays supported on double colonettes. The top storey has only two windows and they may have been a later addition. On top of the cathedral is a sort of onion dome topped by a bell turret.

The base of the tower forms the narthex preceding the nave. The fairly vast interior of the church has ribbed vaulting. The nave has four spans and there are two side aisles. The five-sided chancel extends into two radiating chapels and one side chapel. The vaulted roof is supported on round pillars in the nave and triangular one in the chancel. Superb altar screens, the pulpit and the 17th-century choirstalls serve as a reminder of the fact that this was

The Saint-Sacerdos Cathedral.

The Lantern of the Deceased was built in the 12th Century to commemorate the "miracle of the bread" performed by Saint Bernard, who cured the people of Sarlat of the plague.

OPPOSITE: The La Boétie House,
in which Etienne de La Boétie was born in 1530.

once a cathedral. On the rear of the West Front is an 18th-century loft containing an organ made by Cliquot. The sacristy is in the former chapter house which has a 14th-century ribbed vaulted roof. On the outside, a series of funereal niches dating from the 14th and 16th Centuries can be seen along one side of the apse. Near the cathedral, overlooking a courtyard, is the Blue Penitents' Chapel, a Romanesque church that was altered in the 17th Century.

The former Bishop's Palace adjacent to the cathedral has been restored on several occasions and it is very difficult to date the large mullioned windows on the first floor or the upper gallery built in the Renaissance style. The rear of the building has been turned into a theatre.

The town hall is an elegant 16th and 17th-century building. To one side of the town hall square is the old parish Church of St. Mary dating from the 14th and 15th Centuries. The belltower no longer has a roof. Among the many fine mansions in the town are the Maleville and Plamon Residences and the La Boétie House in which Etienne de La Boétie was born in 1530. The former courthouse has wide bays in the form of a loggia and a lantern turret. The White Penitents' Chapel, originally the chapel used by the Recollects Order, dates from the 17th Century. Its door is in the side wall and is built in the Baroque style. The former Convent of the Poor Clares dating from the 14th to 17th Centuries still has its cloisters.

On the outskirts of the town is the former hospital, a superb 17th-century building which has just been restored.

The 12th-century fortified church in **La Canéda** used to be a preceptory belonging to the Order of the Knights Templar.

To the north of the town, in **Temniac**, is the Chapel of Our Lady. It is a place of pilgrimage but the origins of the pilgrimage are slowly being lost. The Romanesque building includes a vaulted nave with two domes and a five-sided chancel with tunnel vaulting. The interior is decorated with arcading. Outside, the chapel is totally devoid of ornamentation.

All that remains of the former Bishop's Palace that once stood near the chapel is a heap of ruins.

The River Dordogne from Domme.

A trip down the Dordogne Valley

If you leave Sarlat by the south, you will pass the delightful La Boétie Manor before **Domme** slowly becomes visible on the horizon, perched on its rocky promontory more than 487 ft. above the R. Dordogne.

It is from the esplanade in Domme that you can best see the Dordogne Valley. The panoramic view stretches over a distance of several dozen miles and it is easy to begin dreaming of days gone by, when countless heavily-laden barges plied the waterway, between the upper valley and Bordeaux.

The hillside round Domme is riddled with caves which provided the locals with shelter in troubled times. The caves contain some wonderful stalagmites and stalactites and can be reached from the covered market.

Cénac on the banks of the river used to have a priory but it was demolished by the Huguenots, with the exception of the chevet. It has a 12th-century apse with piers, flanked by apsidal chapels with tunnel vaulting. The bays lie between engaged columns. The capitals have elegant carvings.

The church in **Saint-Julien**, which is well-protected by a meander of the R. Dordogne, has a belltower-wall dating

Montfort Castle, much restored during the 19th Century, overlooks the Dordogne from a 295 ft. cliff. At the foot of the castle stretches the largest walnut grove in Europe.

The hilltop town of Domme still has its town walls and fortified gates. Graffiti within the Tower Gate were said to have been left by the Knights Templar.

Domme

Domme is a fortified hilltop town built on the orders of Philip the Bold in 1283 for he had quickly realised the strategic importance of this spot. In fact, there had already been a fortress on the site in earlier years and a few traces of it still remain. Inside the town walls, the layout of the town is less cut-and-dried than in other similar communities because building work had to take account of the lie of the land. There are still three of the old town gates. The Tower Gate (porte des Tours), the largest of the three, is flanked by two round towers with rustication. During occupation by the English army, the soldiers left graffiti on the walls in one of the chambers – or some say that they were the work of the Knights Templar... The Delbos Gate and Combe Gate were defended by slit windows and closed off by a portcullis.

The 16th-century Governor's House stands on the main square opposite the covered market, which has an upper storey. At the corner of the square is the church which was demolished during the Wars of Religion and rebuilt at the start of the 17th Century in accordance with the earlier layout. In the Rue de l'Abbaye, are the remains of a 15th-century cloisters which have now been built into a private house.

Marqueyssac Castle. It is especially interesting for its gardens filled with terraces of box and green oaks said to have been designed by Le Nôtre.

OPPOSITE: La Roque-Gageac.

from the 12th Century. The semi-circular apse is decorated with fine capitals. The church still stands in the middle of its old graveyard.

La Roque-Gageac

La Roque-Gageac is a village strung out between cliffs and the R. Dordogne in a setting so outstanding that it earned the village the title of "the most beautiful village in France". There are countless reminders of its history. Protected by its walls, La Roque never fell into English hands during the One Hundred Years' War, nor into Protestant hands during the Wars of Religion. It became a free town very early on in its history and was governed by Consuls. Its population once rose to fifteen hundred living in what little space there was between its sheer walls of rock and the river, most of them traders or craftsmen, and many of them boatmen for La Roque used to be a flourishing river port.

Yet what time or warfare had not succeeded in destroying was to be suddenly wiped out by Nature. On 17th January 1957 at 10.30 a.m. a gigantic piece of rock detached itself from the cliff face and crashed down, demolishing several houses and causing a number of deaths.

Thanks to an overall plan, the village has now regained its attractiveness with delightful houses roofed with flat tiles that stand out against the yellow ochre of the stone walls. The 16th-century church is perched on the cliff above the village. From the door of the church, there is a superb view.

Tarde Manor, a small mansion built beneath the rock, overlooks the town. This was the birthplace of philosopher Gabriel de Tarde.

Nowadays the fortifications have disappeared and there are no more river boats in the tiny harbour. A new road runs along the river bank, skirting the village. From it, there is a good view of the houses built in terraces up the hillside.

Visitors with a well-developed sense of curiosity will enjoy seeking out the tropical plants that grow on the cliff face thanks to the unusually favourable climatic conditions.

At the entrance to the village is La Malartrie, a pastiche Renaissance mansion built in the latter years of last century. It stands on land that lies within the boundary of the neighbouring village of **Vézac**.

Vézac has no centre as such. Its church, standing alone in the middle of the old graveyard, dates from the 15th-17th Centuries. It has a wonderful stone-slabbed roof.

65

Perched on a crag like an eagle's nest, Beynac Castle towers above the houses huddled at its feet.

Marqueyssac Castle, which was also built on a spur of rock, dates from the 17th Century and is flanked by an engaged round tower. It is especially interesting for its gardens filled with terraces of box and green oaks said to have been designed by Le Nôtre.

Beynac

On the very top of an almost vertical cliff rising from the banks of the R. Dordogne is the proud outline of **Beynac** Castle, often compared to an eagle's nest. Captured and recaptured as a result of countless battles, the castle has had to be rebuilt on several occasions.

The old fortress was the seat of one of the four baronnies in Périgord. It includes a double ring of outer walls overlooking the plateau, while on the south side the cliff face itself constitutes an impregnable system of defence. At the entrance to the first of the outer walls is a barbican.

A huge quadrangular keep with adjacent staircase tower dominates the remainder of the castle. It is topped with crenelations and a small lookout chamber. The keep extends into the main apartments with a machicolated parapet walkway which overlooks a triangular building dating from the 14th Century. From another building to the south, there is a view of the R. Dordogne. This building has stone-mullioned windows whereas the mediaeval sections have double bays.

The vast rooms have been carefully restored and reinforce the general impression of austerity. The Chamber of States, which has ribbed barrel vaulting, was used by the States of Périgord whose members represented all the region's nobility. The private chapel next to the Chamber has frescoes dating from the 15th Century.

Situated at the edge of the outer walls is the village church, once the castle chapel. Built at the same time as the castle, in the 12th Century, it was altered in the 16th. Its stone-slabbed roof bears a belltower wall.

Narrow, steeply-sloping streets run down to the river bank, between houses huddled one up against the other on the cliff face. The frontages bear many a trace of past history.

The former parish of **Cazenac**, now part of the town of Beynac, has a 15th-century Gothic church in which the stained glass windows have been remade by a contemporary artist.

Down from Castelnaud in the Dordogne valley, and opposite Beynac, stands Fayrac Castle.

Les Milandes was the home of the "Children's Village" created by Joséphine Baker for the children she adopted from all over the world. In those days, people would travel from one continent to another just to meet the famous cabaret artist.

OPPOSITE:
The keep in Castelnaud Castle has recently been restored and now houses an interesting museum with exhibits relating to the One Hundred Years' War.

Castelnaud-Fayrac

Standing across the valley from Beynac, **Castelnaud** Castle also kept watch over the exit from the Céou Valley. It was built on a spur of rock and it, too, had to withstand repeated attack from enemy armies.

The castle is partly ruined but its present owners have begun to restore the keep and have already reroofed it. Inside is a museum specialising in the One Hundred Years' War.

Built in the 12th Century, the fortress had to be altered in the 13th and 14th. It still has its original system of fortifications. In front of the castle is a barbican with adjacent tower.

The village also boasts three other splendid residences – Lacoste, Fayrac and Les Milandes.

Lacoste is an elegant 18th and 19th-century mansion surrounded by superb parkland. From it, there is a view over the Dordogne and Céou Valleys.

Fayrac Castle stands on vast earthworks high above the R. Dordogne. Beyond the drawbridge and crenelated barbican stands a fortress, but it underwent major alteration in the 17th and, more particularly, in the 19th Centuries.

Its owner, the musician Fernand de la Tombelle, had an extensive collection of musical instruments. The castle consists of several sections, each linked by towers and turrets.

Les Milandes is best-known as the "home" made by Joséphine Baker for her adopted children from all over the world. The 15th-century castle underwent extensive alterations in the last century. It consists of a vast set of apartments on several floors, with adjacent circular and square towers with stone-slabbed roofs. The windows have mullions rising to finials. The chapel is a graceful Gothic building with a square layout decorated with numerous carvings both outside, on its doorway and piers, and inside.

Beyond Castelnaud Castle lies the Céou Valley which runs up to **Saint-Cybranet, Daglan** and **Bouzic**, picturesque villages on the edge of the département of Lot.

Saint-Cyprien. The church and its belltower-keep.

La Roque Castle, dating from the 15th and 16th Centuries.

Saint-Cyprien

Saint-Cyprien is a small town that grew up in the shadow of an abbey belonging to regular canons of the Augustinian Order.

The church, once the minster, is a Romanesque building with alterations dating from the 14th, 17th and 19th Centuries. It still has its belltower-keep built in the 12th Century, a massive feature that dominates the entire town. Inside, there are some fine fittings including choirstalls, reredos, pulpit, organ and wrought ironwork.

The monastery buildings were used for many years as a tobacco store. One of the buildings has 16th-century Italianate arcading along the top.

Beaumont Manor at the entrance to the town is an elegant 18th-century building. The front is decorated with a triangular pediment over columns.

The houses, with their steeply-sloping roofs, are built up the hillside above the church. One of them is said to have provided accommodation for the English General, Talbot.

Fages Castle, which lies off the beaten track, has benefitted from major restoration over the past few years and has been saved from total ruin as a result.

It stands within a quadrangular outer wall lined with a dry moat that has been partially filled in. In one corner is the half-ruined chapel with its dome and superbly-carved Renaissance doorway. The castle has two sections. One, more austere building has transomed windows; the other dates from the Renaissance period and is topped with machicolations. Wonderful monumental fireplaces set back-to-back in adjacent chambers can be seen on all four floors. Grooved pilasters, capitals decorated with swirls, and triangular or half-moon pediments decorate the Renaissance frontages.

To the north-east of Saint-Cyprien, in **Meyrals**, is La Roque Castle, dating from the 15th and 16th Centuries. It clings onto the hillside above the road. An early 17th-century barbican bars the entrance to the inner courtyard lined with two buildings set at right angles to each other and ending in machicolated towers. The square tower on the south side contains a private chapel decorated with interesting frescoes depicting scenes from the Gospels.

Further up the valley, there is a small road leading through the woods to Redon-Espic Priory. The monastery buildings lie in ruins. The church, though, has ribbed bar-

The covered marketplace in Cadouin in the centre of the square is a reminder of the seasonal fairs and markets which were once held in the town.

rel vaulting built in the purest of proportions. The priory may have been founded, if one is to believe the characteristic layout, by monks from Grandmont. There is an annual pilgrimage to this spot.

Castels still has its old parish church, standing alone and in ruins. Parts of the doorway and Romanesque apse are still visible.

Back in the Dordogne Valley, the road runs along the foot of the remains of Cazelat Castle which lies forgotten in the middle of the forest.

Above the small town of **Mouzens** is Monsec Castle, dating from the 14th and 16th Centuries but with 19th-century alterations. It has two sections set at right angles and ending in towers, one round, the other square. The tall roof is decorated with superb dormer windows.

Where Vézère meets Dordogne

Siorac is overshadowed by the massive outline of its 17th-century castle built in the Classical style. It now houses the town hall.

The tiny village of **Bigaroque** still has the ruins of a castle destroyed during the days of the Wars of Religion. It used to belong to the Bishops of Bordeaux. In the plain, a rather strange tithe barn dating from the 12th and 13th Centuries may have been the place where the Dordogne boatmen came to pay their taxes.

Le Buisson is a recent town which grew up around a railway station. The old parish was situated in Cussac, a hamlet consisting of a few houses and a Romanesque church.

Standing on a hillock above **Le Buisson**, La Bourgonie is a typical Périgord-style manorhouse. Beyond the porch is a square courtyard containing the 16th-century apartments with sloping roof flanked by a staircase tower and, to each side, wings set at right angles to the main building. One of them is an 18th-century country house; the other consists of a roof over massive columns. Outbuildings close off the fourth side of the courtyard.

Cadouin is a small village lost in the middle of the Bessède Forest. Its destiny was closely linked to that of the abbey and the pilgrimage based on the Holy Shroud. Dsicovered in the Holy Land by Adhémar de Monteil during the First Crusade, the Holy Shroud was brought back to Périgord by one of his chaplains. Since then, pilgrimages continued to attract huge crowds. St. Louis himself is said to have come

Cadouin Abbey

The abbey still has all the monastery buildings, making this one of the few surviving examples of a complete Cistercian abbey from that period.

The West Front of the church is austere and powerful, and it forms a striking contrast with the decoration of the apse and apsidal chapels. Inside, there is little decoration, in accordance with the beliefs and traditions of the Cistercian Order. The church has a nave and two side aisles. There is a dome above the transept crossing. In the chancel are a number of frescoes, all extensively restored, depicting the Resurrection of Christ. Two chains from which the Holy Shroud used to hang are still suspended from the vaulted roof.

The belltower is covered with chestnut shingles.

To the south are the 15th and 16th-century cloisters. The four ornate galleries make this one of the finest specimens of Flamboyant Gothic architecture in France. The ribbed arching is elegantly carved, as are the pendentives, countless figures on bosses, and bas-reliefs. The chapter house opens onto the cloisters. It has surbased barrel vaulting. In one of the bedrooms in the vicarage are Aubusson tapestries with motifs taken from La Fontaine's Fables.

The cloisters and bell tower of Cadouin seen from the south gallery.

In the north gallery of Cadouin cloisters, there still remains the bench where the monks used to sit, with the abbot's throne in the centre. The gallery is decorated with highly-intricate sculptures (this is a close-up of one of them).

to pray before the relic but, in 1934, after meticulous examination of the piece of cloth, the pilgrimage was abandoned.

Turning back towards the R. Dordogne, we arrive in Limeuil, where the R. Vézère flows into the Dordogne, thereafter forming a single waterway. There are two right-angled bridges across the river, and there is a splendid view of the town from them.

The Limeuil and Trémolat Meanders

The R. Dordogne twists and turns, forming meanders without ever coming right back on itself. These deep meanders are known locally as "cingles"; they are graceful quirks of nature. On one side, the river laps the base of sheer cliffs that provide a natural rampart against any flooding; on the other side, the land encircled by the meander is particularly suitable for farming.

The best way to see the Limeuil and Trémolat meanders is to follow the hilltop route. From there, you have a panoramic view that changes with the seasons, forming a symphony of colours that is a delight to the eye.

Limeuil used to be a walled town with fortifications but

Saint Martin's church, at the foot of the town of Limeuil, dates from the 12th Century and has a narthex topped by a dome.

Trémolat was the seat of an influential abbey which is said to have been given a relic by Charlemagne – a shirt worn by the Infant Jesus.

only three gates now remain. The houses huddle close to each other, on terraces along the cliff face. At the top is a 12th-century castle that is now all but in ruins.

The village church was renovated in the 19th Century but it still has its 14th-century chancel. The former Recollects Convent, built in the 17th Century, lies on the river bank.

Set apart some distance from the village, is St. Martin's Church, a 12th-century Romanesque buildings with some fine carved modillions. The transept crossing has a dome over pendentives. The West Front has a doorway with coving.

Trémolat is closely linked to the story of St. Cybard who was said to have been born here in the 6th Century. Charlemagne is said to have gifted a relic to the newly-created monastery – a shirt said to have belonged to the Child Jesus which was held aloft so that the congregation could pray to it.

The monastery developed under Benedictine Rule. The church is the former minster. It was built in the shape of a Latin Cross with a first span under the belltower, a four-span nave but no side aisles, a projecting transept and a very elongated chancel. The nave is roofed with a succession of domes, while the chancel and arms of the transept have barrel vaulting. The side walls are strengthened by buttresses.

The outside is dominated by the fortified belltower. In the 18th Century, the doorway was given Classical decoration.

In the graveyard stands the old parish church, dedicated to St. Hilary. The doorway, beneath a cornice supported on seven carved modillions, is highlighted by a triple row of coving and an archivolt supported on colonettes.

At the end of the Trémolat Meander are the remains of **Badefols** Castle, a reminder of the demands made by Séguin de Badefols, a famous 14th-century gang leader. The church, built in the 17th-18th Centuries, used stone from the former Church of St. Vincent of Viralet and from the Protestant church that had been demolished on Louis XIV's orders.

The tiny church in Saint-Front-de-Colubri overlooking Lalinde keeps alive the memory of St. Front who hunted down the coloubre, a legendary creature said to have devoured the Dordogne's boatmen.

The papermills

The Couze Valley was, for many centuries, one of the most active paper-making centres of South-Western France. There were no less than two papermills in what we now know as Couze and Bayac.

At regular intervals, huge loads of paper were loaded onto barges and taken down the R. Dordogne to Bordeaux where they were despatched to Northern Europe.

The papermills, which can still be seen today, have a very characteristic layout. They vary in length depending on output but from the outside their purpose is obvious because of the treble that filled the entire upper storey. In the large chamber on the first floor, the sheets were sorted and counted before being stamped with the mill's own mark. The ground floor or, in some cases the cellar, contained the rooms in which the rags were prepared, left to rot, placed in vats, and pressed. In many cases, they also contained the beater.

The papermill also included accommodation and service premises.

The paper-making tradition has been kept alive by recent mills and by a craftsman who continues to make paper by hand. A paper museum has also been opened in one of the old mills.

OPPOSITE:
Villefranche-du-Périgord. The covered market.

Lalinde and the Couze Valley

Lalinde is an English hilltop town, founded in the 13th Century. It was a major river port, as shown by the canal that bears its name and runs parallel to the R. Dordogne.

Like all hilltop towns, it has a checkerboard layout. It still has some of its town walls and one of the gates, the Roman Gate.

On the other bank of the river is the Chapel of Saint-Front-de-Colubri, a 12th-century Romanesque building. It was dedicated to St. Front, the apostle of Périgord who came here to hunt down the coulobre, a legendary monster that devoured boatmen.

Standing on a spur of rock above the R. Couze, Bannes Castle was built in the 16th Century. It has an irregular layout and its mighty towers contrast sharply with the elegance of its Renaissance frontage. The doors and windows are decorated with delicate carvings.

The hilltop villages

In French, they are called "bastides" but just what exactly are they? The French word comes from the ancient word "bastida" meaning a wooden tower then, in the Middle Ages, a system of defence. This meant that the bastides were built for defensive purposes. Yet from the early 13th Century onwards, the term applied more often to a new town or settlement. Most of them were defended by fortifications.

From the outset, the towns were built to a rigorous checkerboard pattern, with streets cutting across each other at right angles. Generally speaking, the church was built in one corner of the central square. It is open to debate whether the arcades that line the square were built at the same time as the town or added on at a later date.

Twenty-five such hilltop towns were set up in Périgord but, in fact, there are only eighteen real bastides there today. They were all built in a little over fifty years between 1250 (Villefranche-du-Périgord) and 1316 (Saint-Barthélémy).

Most of these towns were built on the orders of the Kings of England. The others were commissioned by the Kings of France or Alphonse of Poitiers. Only rarely was the decision taken by a local nobleman.

To the north of the département, between the rivers Dordogne and Dronne, hilltop towns are few in number.

Beaumont-du-Périgord is one of the many hilltop towns in Périgord. It still has part of its system of defence. The large awe-inspiring church stands at one corner of the main square.

The Bailie's House is in Molières, a 13th-century English hilltop town which was never completed.

Monpazier is one of the best-preserved of all the hilltop towns. Its ordered design with streets set at right angles to each other is typical of the new towns of south-west France founded in the 13th Century.

The square in the centre of Monpazier has a series of arcades on all four sides. The covered market still has its set of measures.

They are **Vergt, Beauregard, Saint-Louis, Bénévent, Saint-Barthélémy, Saint-Aulaye,** and **Villefranche-du-Périgord.** This means that most of the bastides lie in the south of the département, many of them in the Dropt Valley. The same applies to the adjoining départements of Gironde and Lot-et-Garonne, giving Aquitaine, with its rural villages and mediaeval places of sanctuary, one of the most characteristic features of its population density and housing.

We have already visited the bastides of Domme and Lalinde.

Beaumont-du-Périgord was English and still has some interesting old buildings. The central square has only three sides left; it is lined with arcaded houses. Other 12th and 14th-century houses can be seen in the old streets. Little remains of the town walls except a few stretches of masonry. The fortified Luzier Gate still has the groove in which the portcullis was raised and lowered. St. Front's Church was built as the final line of defence. On the outside, there are four defensive towers flanking the West Front and chevet. A parapet walkway runs along the top of its walls. The church has a basket doorway beneath a ribbed arch with five rows of coving. Inside, the six spans were reroofed in modern times.

Biron Castle, situated on the borders of Dordogne and Lot-et-Garonne, consists of several buildings dating from the 12th to 17th Centuries. It was the seat of one of Périgord's four baronies.

Molières, which was also built by the English, was left unfinished. It has a checkerboard layout converging on the central square. Only the so-called "Bailie's House" has its arcades. There are superb double windows on the front. The fortified church seems to be excessively large for such a small village. It has a massive belltower on the north side. The church was built in the Gothic style and has ribbed vaulting.

Monpazier was founded by the Kings of France and is doubtless the best-preserved of all Périgord's hilltop towns. It is often mentioned because of its perfect layout and the quality of its buildings. Three of the original six gates are still in position today. The central square is lined with wonderful arcades, all of them different. The covered market contains a complete series of grain measures. The Chapter House, a tall building three storeys high, was used, despite its name, as the tithe barn. The church, on which building began at the same time as the village itself, was altered in later years. Beside the doorway is a funereal niche. The nave has four spans with ribbed arching supported by engaged columns. The five-side apse was added on in the 15th Century. **Monestier** has the regular layout of streets and a few houses with arcades.

Right in the south of the area is **Villefranche-du-Périgord**, again commissioned by the Kings of France. It is a superb town. The streets are lined with old houses and other reminders of times past and all of them cut across each other at right angles. The general layout is like a chckerboard. The central square still has a row of arcades. On one side is the covered market, which comes alive during the mushroom-picking season. It still has its set of grain measures. The rafters are supported by stone pillars.

At the other end of the region is **Eymet**, a French bastide which has retained its original layout. The central square is flanked by arcades. Some stretches of the old town walls are still visible. All that remains of the old castle is the square 14th-century keep, usually known as the Monseigneur Tower.

Little remains of the other hilltop towns i.e. **Roquépine**, **Fonroque** or **Puyguilhem**.

Biron

Biron is one of the four baronnies of Périgord. After a long history of grandeur and abject poverty, it was divided up by its last owners before being bought back by the département and systematically restored.

Biron Castle.

It is gradually regaining its erstwhile lustre and now, perched on its hillock, it contemplates the surrounding area, from Monpazier to the edge of the Agen region. This is a well-preserved area that seems to have stepped straight out of the pages of a history book.

The castle has a complex layout. It includes buildings from various periods ranging from the 12th to the 18th Centuries and there has been no attempt to ensure symmetry.

The castle gradually lost its system of defence, which once included two outer walls with moat. The castle walls were opened up and bay windows included, overlooking the surrounding countryside. Beyond the entrance is a barbican with piers decorated with mullioned windows. It is extended by a sort of loggia high above the curtain wall and running into the chapel.

The chapel is two storeys high. Around its tall slate roof is a promenade with a traceried balustrade. The chapel was reserved for the lord and his family or friends, on the level with the courtyard. It has ribbed vaulting and contains the tombs of Pons and Armand de Gontaut. On the lower level, the chapel was used as a parish church by the inhabitants of the adjacent village.

A small manorhouse known as the Tax Pavilion consisting of two interlinked houses also opens onto the first courtyard. A flight of steps leads up to the upper level.

This is the main courtyard. A series of apartments with mullioned windows back onto a square Romanesque keep with flat piers. At one end of the courtyard is a wide portico supported on a surbased arch on one side and on double columns on the outside.

The building as a whole is further adorned with Renaissance dormer windows, cornices, and moulding, making it one of the most attractive castles in Périgord.

The tiny village, with houses backing directly onto the former ramparts, entwines itself round the hillock, at the foot of the castle.

Further down still is another small village, outside the walls. It has its own church, Notre-Dame-sous-Biron, a fine Romanesque building dating from the 12th Century. Opposite it is a house said to have belonged to Bernard Palissy, the famous master glass-painter and potter.

Sainte-Croix Church.

**Monferrand.
The Gothic chapel.**

On the edge of the Bessède Forest

The abbey of **Saint-Avit-Sénieur** was built near the grave of Avit, a former soldier who became a hermit. The church was consecrated in 1117. At the end of the 12th Century, the abbey was entrusted to the canons of the Augustinian Order.

On the outside, the buildings are fairly austere. The West Front of the church is flanked by two towers interlinked by a parapet walkway. Inside, the nave has three spans with ribbed vaulting; there are no side aisles. The chevet wall was rebuilt in the 14th Century and, in the 17th, a large bay window was made in it. The keystones represent a hand raised in blessing, a bishop and a Paschal lamb.

As far as the abbey buildings are concerned, all that remains is the site of the cloisters, and the chapter house. A small archaeological museum has been opened on the upper storey. Following the discovery of graves of pilgrims on their way to Santiago de Compostela, memorabilia relating to this pilgrimage was laid out in a small room on the ground floor. A two-storey building with a double gallery lies in the second courtyard where numerous substructures of other buildings have been brought to light.

Sainte-Croix was the seat of a priory but the buildings are almost in ruins. It has twin windows separated by a colonnette. The other walls contain mullioned windows (15th Century) and 18th-century bays.

The church is a fairly large Romanesque building with a semi-circular porch. The nave and south aisle have barrel vaulting. Above the transept crossing is a dome over pendentives. The apse is semi-circular. The arches are supported on carved capitals.

Beyond the small town is Sainte-Croix House, a vast residence built in the 17th and 18th Centuries. A monumental gateway leads into a large, enclosed courtyard with the mansion on one side.

Montferrand is dominated by the remains of a fortress that was destroyed during the One Hundred Years' War and the Wars of Religion. Its present owners have begun restoring part of the buildings. The remains of the outer wall, square keep and 16th-century apartments are still visible.

In the village, the 16th-century covered market is surrounded by old houses, some of them with balconies and dovecots.

There is a Gothic chapel in the cemetery containing a number of very fine frescoes.

The Recollects Convent in Bergerac is now the home of the Bergerac Wine Centre which monitors the quality of these highly-esteemed wines.

The wines of Bergerac

The wines of Bergerac enjoyed a good reputation very many years ago. They include both reds and whites, among the latter, Monbazillac, which is in a class of its own. It is a sweet, golden wine with a full flavour and is ideal as an aperitif or served with foie gras or a desert. Its unusual bouquet is due to the so-called "noble rot" which reduces the acidity in the grapes.

The red wines, the Bergeracs or Côtes de Bergeracs, have a full, fruity flavour and can be drunk young. The more robust Pécharmants should be left to age in a good cellar.

The semi-sweet whites i.e. Côtes de Bergarac, Rosette, Saussignac, and Côtes de Montravel, should be served as an aperitif or with desert. The dry whites, Bergeracs or Montravels, are an ideal accompaniment for seafood or fish.

Mounet-Sully House on the outskirts of Bergerac was built at the turn of the century for the famous tragic actor.

Bergerac is a market town on the banks of the R. Dordogne. Saint James' Church (église Saint-Jacques) stands in the centre of the old town on the edge of the Place Pélissière.

Bergerac in Purple Périgord

Standing fairly and squarely on the banks of the Dordogne, **Bergerac** is a river port although, after centuries of bustle, its quaysides have now become much quieter. Their beautiful cobblestones now form a car park.

Bergerac's history began during the days of the Roman Occupation. Once encircled by walls, the town also suffered during times of war, especially during the Wars of Religion because Bergerac was a major centre of the Protestant faith, as it still is today. The John Bost Foundation on the outskirts of the town is one of the Reformed Church's largest reception and care centres.

Although Bergerac was a busy trading and commercial centre, it did not acquire the historic buildings we have seen in other towns in the Périgord region. Yet strenuous efforts over the past few years have resulted in improvements to the St. James' District (quartier Saint-Jacques).

A stroll through the narrow streets in this district gives visitors a chance to see half-timbered houses with earth or shingle filling, and other houses with mediaeval bays or Renaissance windows, turrets, and large timber balconies that form a sort of gallery overlooking the courtyard.

Among them is the Peyrarède Residence at the street corner, still known today as Henri IV's castle because the king is said to have stayed there. There is also the old inn, a house with arcades which, like the other example given, dates from the 17th Century. Near the quayside is an old grain store, a proud building several storeys high. On the banks of the Dordogne is a late 18th-century house that has been turned into a clinic.

St. James' Church (église Saint-Jacques) is the parish church of Old Bergerac. Built in the 11th Century, it had to be rebuilt in the 14th and 17th Centuries and was then renovated again last century. A recent restoration project has succeeded in bringing to light the oldest parts of the building. The chancel has fittings from the same period.

Across the bridge is the Church of St. Mary Magdalen (église de la Madeleine), which dates from the early years of the 19th Century. As to Notre-Dame Church, it was built in later years, in the Neo-Gothic style. It was designed by Abadie, the famous architect, and is undoubtedly one of the most interesting buildings of its time.

The Protestant church stands on the site of the erstwhile Recollects convent. The adjacent cloisters have a double

Monbazillac Castle overlooks the vineyards which are famed throughout the world.

Monbazillac

Monbazillac stands stoically overlooking the vineyards that grow in terraces right down the hillside and into the valley. Built in the 16th Century, it is a large rectangle flanked at each corner by a round tower. Austere dormer windows jut up from the parapet walkway that runs right round the building. The windows have stone transoms. In the out-buildings, the Monbazillac cooperative wine cellar which owns the residence has laid out a wine-tasting room. It has also created a museum devoted to the Protestant faith.

wooden gallery dating from the Renaissance period. One of the galleries was brought here from an old house in Bergerac.

The cloisters, and what remains of the convent buildings, are the head offices of the Centre Interprofessionnel des Vins de Bergerac (C.I.V.R.B, the Bergerac Wine Centre). Solemn enrollment ceremonies are held in the cellars, giving people an opportunity to find out more about the region's wines.

Castles in the vineyards

To the north of Bergerac is Garrigues Castle, now better-known as Mounet-Sully after its builder. This was considered by Jean Secret as "the cheekiest and most whimsical of all the castles in Périgord". It combines every possible period, juxtaposing willy-nilly Romanesque, Gothic or Renaissance features, setting a lookout tower next to a patio and a bartizan. It is rather like a theatrical backdrop and is characteristic of Mounet-Sully who was one of the greatest artistes at the turn of the century.

In the same town is Lespinassat Castle consisting of a vast main section with 17th-century frontage to the south and

Pile Castle on the banks of the R. Dordogne has an interesting Renaissance façade.

ABOVE, RIGHT:
Montastruc Castle combines 16th and 17th-century buildings which stand on 13th-century foundations.

OPPOSITE:
Gageac Castle is surrounded by a crenelated wall with a parapet walkway and corner watchtowers.

18th-century frontage to the north. A horseshoe-shaped staircase leads from the entrance up to the first floor topped by a triangular pediment. The north wall is flanked by two pavilions which were connected to the main apartments in the 19th Century. The buildings are surrounded by a moat.

In **Cours-de-Pile**, the castle is an elegant 16th-century building with towers that are reflected in the waters of the R. Dordogne. It has a superb Renaissance frontage.

On a terrace high above the R. Dordogne is Tiregant House which has 18th and 19th-century buildings.

Bridoire Castle in **Ribagnac** was built over foundations dating from the 12th Century. It comprises two main buildings (15th and 16th Centuries) set at right angles to each other. Four machicolated towers stand at each of the projecting corners. The castle has windows with stone transoms. The interior is in a very poor state of repair as a result of vandalism. Father de Foucault stayed in the castle on several occasions.

Issigeac was once a walled ecclesiastical town. The Bishop's Palace stands on one side, with a vast 17th-century building flanked by two corner pavilions with corbelled turrets. The church was built in the Late Gothic style. The

nave and side aisles have ribbed vaulting. The chevet is five-sided.

In **Gageac-Rouillac**, Gageac Castle replaced a 14th-century fortress. The central building flanked by machicolated corner towers extends into wings set at right angles to it.

Saussignac is a vast 17th-century mansion. The central part of the house, which stands between two corner pavilions, has never been completed. The two wings set at right angles to the main section have Mansard roofs.

Let us now slow down a little for there are many other mansions and castles with character adorning the countryside around Bergerac and they are well worth a closer look.

Montaigne and Gurson

In **Montcaret**, archaeological digs undertaken in the last century revealed major Gallo-Roman remains. It would seem that a succession of villas was built on the site from the first to the fifth century. They were followed by a Benedictine priory which, in the 11th Century, was replaced by the church we see today. The apse and apsidal chapels are original. Some of the capitals are Gallo-Roman carvings which were re-used in the church.

Michel de Montaigne loved to retire amidst his books in the Library Tower, where he would write and meditate.

Saint-Michel de Montaigne is, needless to say, the birthplace of the great philospher, Montaigne. The library tower still exists today. It is cylindrical in shape and the ground floor was the philosopher's chapel. A small lodge enabled him to follow the service without having to leave his apartments. Upstairs is the library in which the ceiling was painted with Latin and Greek mottos selected by Montaigne himself.

Nothing now remains of the castle in which Michel Eyquem lived. It had to be rebuilt in the middle of the 19th Century for its then owner, Pierre Magne, a government minister, after being destroyed by fire.

The ruins of Gurson Castle still stand proudly at the top of its feudal motte. Remains of the keep, barbican and main apartments are still visible.

The area around Gurson has a particularly large number of Romanesque churches in which the decorative features are reminiscent of the churches in the Saintonge area. In **Carsac de Gurson**, for example, the church doorway has six lines of coving supported on colonettes and pilasters. To each side is semi-circular blind arcading supported on colonettes. Above the doorway is a carved cornice on modillions.

It bears five arches separated by colonettes and pilasters. The capitals are all carved. The nave has a barrel vaulted roof; the apse has tunnel vaulting.

Saint-Martin-de-Gurson also has a superb 12th-century church built in the style of the Saintonge area.

Mathecoulon Castle overlooks the valley and once belonged to Montaigne's brother. The residence we see today dates from the 17th and 18th Centuries and was built in the shape of a 'U'. Above the entrance is a pediment and a circular roof.

The church in **Montpeyroux** is particularly outstanding. Although it is small, it has a barrel-vaulted nave, a false transept with a dome over pendentives, and a rounded apse. Above the church is a square belltower. The West Front and apse are decorated with more than one hundred modillions. Opposite the church are the remains of a priory.

Villefranche-de-Lonchat was an English hilltop town. It still has its characteristic layout with streets cutting across each other at right angles. On the edge of the central square is St. Anne's Chapel (14th Century). It has ribbed vaulting. Also overlooking the square is a mid 19th-century building topped by a lantern turret. It now houses the

A Gothic chapel, serving as a parish church, stands in the centre of the hilltop town of Villefranche-de-Lonchat.

Montaigne's Tower still has the atmosphere and furniture the Périgord philosopher wished for. Here the "Library" whose beams have been covered with Latin and Greek proverbs.

town hall and a small local history museum. Traces of the old castle can still be seen on a number of houses.

The church in Villefranche stands outside the walled town. It has three aisles dating from the 14th and 15th Centuries. The pentagonal apse has ribbed vaulting.

The Landais area

This is a very distinct region, similar in some ways to the Double area which we will see later, as we travel north of the Isle Valley.

The soil, a mixture of sand, gravel and clay, is ideal for the thick forests. After the First World War, resinous timber fetched astronomical prices and tapping was a commonplace activity. It had begun in the early years of the previous century and had given this small region its name, a reminder of the huge Landes area on the shores of the Atlantic.

Economic resources have always been limited here. Housing, usually built in clearings, is traditionally made of timber and earth. The villages such as **Bosset**, **Lunas** or **Ginestet** are small.

Over the centuries, this area became the haunt of brigands and the socially-deprived.

Montréal

Beyond the town of Issac is Montréal Castle, standing on a spur of rock high above the valley. It consists of a rectangular building flanked by a circular tower. The windows are Renaissance with transoms and mullions. It still has part of its outer wall, sections of which date back to the 11th Century.

The chapel is an elegant 16th-century building with a staircase turret to one side. Inside it is a relic of the Holy Thorn said to have been found on the body of General Talbot after the Battle of Castillon.

The Canadian city of Montreal got its name from the Lord of Montréal, Claude de Pontbriand, who accompanied Jacques Cartier on his voyage to Canada.

The Vergt area

The Vergt area forms a vast triangle with its apex south of Périgueux, its sides along the roads to Bergerac and Les Eyzies and its base lying up against the Liorac Forest. Over the past few years, it has enjoyed an economic revival thanks to strawberry farming.

Vergt is a bastide, founded in 1290 by King Edward I with the Count of Périgord, Archambaud III. It has retained its characteristic layout but the buildings date from later periods.

In **Saint-Laurent-des-Bâtons**, St. Maurice' Castle is an attractive 15th and 16th-century building with machicolations. The nearby church is a Gothic building with 16th-century alterations.

Clermont-de-Beauregard was a fortified town in the Middle Ages. A few ruins of the mediaeval castle can still be seen today, including a 15th-century staircase tower with a modern statue of the Virgin Mary on the top. Opposite the castle is La Gaubertie, a 15th and 16th-century mansion. Its main section includes an upper floor and it is flanked by a square tower to one side and a corbelled turret to the other. There is a cylindrical tower adjacent to the opposite wall. A parapet walkway over machicolations runs right round the building.

On the edge of a plateau high above the Louyre Valley is Longas Castle in **Sainte-Foy-de-Longas**, dating from the 15th Century. It still has its apartments and machicolated towers.

Sainte-Alvère further east once stood within the walls of the Lostanges family castle but it was methodically destroyed by Lakanal during the French Revolution. There are, though, still a few of the towers from the outer wall and a monumental gateway. The village underwent major changes last century as the result of a road-building programme.

The Crempse Valley

Beauregard is an old hilltop town founded by King Edward I in 1268. The covered market still stands on the main square. In Bassac, the small Romanesque church was once a place of pilgrimage in honour of Our Lady.

People tended to pass through **Pont-Saint-Mamet** rather than stop there but even so it was feared by travellers because of its layout. For many years, the gendarmerie

Mathecoulon Castle is an elegant dwelling flanked by two pavilions set at right angles to it dating from the 17th and 18th Centuries. It was owned by a brother of Montaigne.

ABOVE, RIGTH:
Neuvic-Mellet Castle.

OPPOSITE:
Beauregard is an unfinished hilltop town which has a fine covered market supported by stone pillars.

had its main station in the small town. Saint-Mamet Castle is a 17th-century manorhouse flanked by outbuildings forming a courtyard. On the hillside opposite is Lestaubière Castle (19th Century).

Saint-Hilaire-d'Estissac has an 11th-century church with a dome. The apse is semi-circular. La Rigaudie is a prime example of a 17th-century Périgord gentleman's country residence.

La Ponsie in Saint-Jean-d'Estissac is a Renaissance house with carved gable ends and an adjacent staircase tower. Outbuildings and the old chapel lie beyond the main apartments. This was the birthplace of Father Fénelon, nephew of the "Swan of Cambrai". He was almoner to Marie-Antoinette and was beheaded during the French Revolution.

As you drive along the valley, you will see other old mansions. Some of them were the homes of foundry owners, for the banks of the R. Crempse were dotted with countless foundries and mills.

Here we are, though, in Mussidan, in the Isle Valley.

The Isle Valley

Saint Astier has enjoyed a period of development over the past few years and the new urban districts snake out far along the valley. The town centre lies adjacent to the church. It includes old half-timbered houses and Renaissance mansions.

The church is dominated by its square belltower dating from the 15th and 16th Centuries. The corners of the building are strengthened with piers. The nave has ribbed vaulting. The crypt dates from the 11th Century. There are defensive features around the top of the walls.

Further north is Puyferrat Castle, a 16th-century house with corbelled turrets on one side ad two large circular towers on the other. There is a parapet walkway beneath the tall roof.

Neuvic Castle dates from the Renaissance period. It consists of two buildings set at right angles to each other. The square tower in the corner contains the staircase. The wide windows have stone mullions. A parapet walkway runs right round the building. Dormer windows with pointed gables project from the roof.

On the hillside on the other side of the main road is

Frateau Castle. Inside what was once an outer wall is a 15th-century house with extensive later alterations. Much has been done to save the building from what appeared to be inevitable ruin. It now houses a small pottery museum. A small stream wends its way beneath the buildings and terrace.

Mauriac Castle, which lies within the boundaries of **Douzillac**, also dates from the 16th Century. Built on the site of an older castle, it is rectangular in shape with two round machicolated towers. In front of it is a barbican.

Sourzac has the remains of an old priory. The church stands high above the river. It has a ribbed vaulted roof. Near the belltower-keep are the remains of an earlier church. The Gabillou Cave contains a number of paintings dating from the Magdalanian Era.

Mussidan has been a small commercial town since 1497 when the first fairs and markets were organised here. It once had a fortress but Richelieu ordered its demolition in 1624 and little now remains of it. On the outskirts of the town is the Voulgre Museum, a collection of regional art housed in an elegant country house.

Saint-Martin-l'Astier has an isolated church dating from the 12th Century. It is fairly unusual in that it has an octagonal chancel surrounded by columns.

In **Vauclaire**, you can see the buildings of what was once the Carthusian monastery. It has been turned into a psychiatric hospital. The Gothic chapel has been preserved, as have the cloisters.

By the time we reach **Montpont**, another small commercial town, we are on the edge of Périgord and Gironde, and well on the way to Bordeaux, the region's main city.

The Double area

The Double area, like the Landais, is often compared to Sologne. It has the same clay and sand soil that gives the landscape its unusual appearance.

Clearly bordered by the rivers Isle and Dronne, this is an area of untamed countryside dotted with lakes, where forests predominate. Housing is built only in clearings. This used to be a very unhealthy area in which to live and brigands and wild animals found it much to their liking. Because of this, the area had a reputation as a dangerous place and people avoided travelling through it if they could travel round it by taking a different route.

It was "a poor area with poor housing for poor people". Most of the houses were built of timber and earth. Stone was used only for house fronts and even then only in housing built for the wealthier members of society. Most of the farms consisted of one or two rooms for the family, a barn, and an oven. In Le Parcot, the La Double Folk Museum is housed in one of these old dwellings.

In the mid 19th Century, a special effort was made to open up this area. Roads were built, soil improvement was carried out, the land was drained and, at the same time, maritime pines were planted. Gradually, living conditions began to change. Fish farming has also been developed thanks to the many lakes in the locality.

The arrival of Trappist monks also changed the way of life. They cleared land, introduced new crops, used updated farming methods, and succeeded in changing the way of life. Although the monks have since left the area, they have been replaced in Echourgnac Abbey by nuns who still make the famous Trappe cheese.

The small villages all huddle round their church. In **La Jemaye**, for example, the few houses line the road. Further down the hill is a covered market with a vast expanse of roof supported on wooden pillars. The chevet in the church is Romanesque; the remainder dates from last century.

Most of the churches are small. Many of them are Romanesque but most were altered at the turn of the century, reflecting the new development of the area as a whole. This was particularly true in **Servanches, Saint-Michel-de-Double** or **Saint-André-de-Double**.

La Rigale still has its Gallo-Roman tower, a small-scale replica of the Vesuna Tower in Périgueux.

The R. Dronne flows through some enchanting places of outstanding beauty, such as here between the villages of Villetoureix and Saint-Martial-de-Ribérac.

Opposite, top: Parcot farm, in the heart of the Double area, offers both an introduction to, and an insight into, the local environment and lifestyle.

Opposite, bottom: The nave of Ribérac's old church has been restored to its original level. The Romanesque apse at the far end still has some 17th-century paintings.

There are few castles here, and the ones that do exist are also of modest proportions. In many cases, they were the homes of master glass-makers, as was the La Molle Manor in **Eygurande-et-Gardedeuil** or La Devize Manor, an 18th-century house in **Saint-Barthélemy-de-Bellegarde**.

Vanxains at the northern tip of the area is already a precursor of the Ribérac area. The village has a set of old houses, many of them with upper storeys. The remains of the castle can be seen in the cetre of the village. There is one tower beside the façade and, overlooking the innter courtyard, stone-mullioned windows in the other façade. The domed church dates from the 12th Century. The upper section is fortified. Inside, there are some outstanding carved capitals.

Ribérac in White Périgord
Ribérac is an old town on the banks of the R. Dronne and is now a shopping and administrative centre.

The town's origins can be dated back to the Viking invasions. At Le Chalard, the place at which travellers passed through this area, fortifications were built in 866 A.D on the orders of Wilgrin, Count of Périgord and Angoumois.

When peace returned, Alchier-the-Deaf, the Count's representative, is said to have moved uphill and ordered the building of Ribérac Castle.

Increasing numbers of houses were then built close up to the walls of the castle and the town was born.

The castle was the birthplace of Arnaud Daniel, a troubadour who was the protegee of both Richard the Lionheart and Alfonso of Aragon.

Nothing is left of the castle, except a drawing by Léo Drouyn showing the large expanse of ruins that existed at the end of last century. Everything has since disappeared. Houses have been built along what was once the outer wall.

The old Notre-Dame Church probably replaced the original castle chapel when the collegiate church of Ribérac was founded in 1500.

This church, which is now no longer used for services, has become an exhibition and concert hall after a complete restoration. The chancel and apse date from the 12th Century. The chancel has a dome over pendentives. The nave and side aisles were renovated in 1836. The West Front is topped by a rounded pediment. Frescoes can be seen in the chancel and on the ceiling in the nave.

Faye, which was a parish in its own right until the French Revolution, has a small Romanesque church. The tympanum on the West Front bears a carving of Christ in Glory with two angels pouring incense over him. The nave has wooden rafters. The narthex has a barrel-vaulted roof and the semi-circular apse has tunnel vaulting. The apse is surrounded by colonettes in groups of three. On the outside of the building, semi-circular arches decorate the chevet.

Saint-Martial-de-Ribérac was another parish and it, too, was annexed to Ribérac during the French Revolution. Its church is hardly visible in the midst of the houses. The West Front has a semi-circular door with three rows of coving above it. The chancel has a barrel-vaulted roof.

As it runs up the right bank of the R. Dronne, the road skirts the foot of the town of **Villetoureix**, standing in the shadow of the impressive modern belltower on its church. A short distance away is the Gallo-Roman Rigale Tower, all that remains of a cella. This is a replica of the Vesuna Tower in Périgueux, but it is smaller. On the east side, a building with an upper floor was built into the tower in the 17th Century.

On the other side of the R. Dronne, picturesque villages seem to have escaped the passage of time. **Douchapt** huddles round its Romanesque church. **Saint-Pardoux-de-Drône**, which existed in Roman times, has a Romanesque church which was altered during the Gothic period. **Segonzac** has two castles, one dating from the 17th and 18th Centuries and the other, La Martinie, an elegant manorhouse built in the 14th Century and altered in the 17th.

Tocane lies further east and is thought to be an old bastide which merged with the parish of **Saint-Apre**. Above the village is Fayolle Castle, a large 18th-century building that was further extended in the 19th. Built over a small stream, it includes a romantic theatre. Beauséjour Manor on the banks of the R. Dronne was the birthplace of Fénelon's mother.

Domed churches

Churches with domes or even rows of domes are one of the characteristic features of the Ribérac area. It is true that there are others to be seen elsewhere in Périgord but it is in and around Ribérac that they are most commonplace and it is probably this area that has the oldest of such sanctuaries.

Decorative features are less abundant than in the Angoulême area and often consist of the same motifs. The walls, though, were covered in paintings, with scenes from the Old and New Testaments like the ones that can still be seen in **Bourg-du-Bost**.

Let us take a closer look at some of these churches.

The side portal of Grand-Brassac church has an interesting decor, including a few traces of polychromy.

OPPOSITE:
The remains of the Tour Blanche fortress have seen many changes of fortune over the centuries.

Grand-Brassac has a semi-circular window and a Gothic doorway in the West Front. A defensive chamber with crenelations protects the entrance. The North wall is decorated with double arcading, again topped by battlements. One of the doors has been decorated with ornamentation reused from earlier times; it includes several figures. The south wall is more austere. The belltower-keep is in the centre of the building. It is decorated with arcading and topped with crenelations.

Inside the three-span nave has domes over pendentives supported on a transverse rib. The Romanesque windows are set deep into the walls. The building dates from the 12th and 13th Centuries.

In **Paussac**, the church has two domes covering the two spans in the nave. The 13th-century chancel was given a dome over pendentives at a later date; it is smaller than the others. The belltower stands above the chancel crossing.

The West Front has a porch extending into a semi-circular bay. The north wall has regularly-spaced flat piers. The south wall has two great arches supported on columns. Beneath a string-course are four arches in pairs. They are built inside the others and are supported by colonettes.

90

The church in **Cherval** has a Romanesque nave under a row of four domes. The side walls have been decorated with four great Gothic load-bearing arches.

Villetoureix has a church with two domes but one of them is modern.

In the centre of the village of **Siorac-de-Ribérac** high above a valley is a fortified Romanesque church topped by a belltower-keep dating from the 14th Century which was added on to the square belltower built in the 12th Century. The nave has one dome over pendentives. A vaulted passageway runs along the western wall.

The church in **Cumond** underwent extensive alterations last century. It too has a dome above the nave. Behind the church is Cumond Castle, a vast Classical house with an upper storey and a Mansard roof.

The church in **Saint-Privat-des-Prés** is one of the most interesting Romanesque churches in Périgord because it has remained almost unaltered since it was built. The West Front has a semi-circular doorway with nine rows of coving, flanked by two rows of blind arcading. On the upper section, a row of blind arcading is supported on colonettes. The side walls are decorated with arcading that include windows.

The triple-span nave has ribbed barrel vaulting supported on massive arches. There is a dome above the transept crossing. The chevet is flat.

These, though, are only some of the domed churches. There are many others waiting to be discovered in the Ribérac area.

Castles in the Mareuil area

The Mareuil area boasts a particularly large number of castles and old houses. Most of them belonged to vineyard owners until the early years of this century.

Mareuil Castle was the seat of one of the four baronnies in Périgord, with Bourdeilles, Beynac and Biron. It is built in the plain and is surrounded by a double row of walls flanked by towers.

A fortified postern gate opens onto the first courtyard. The second entrance is flanked by two round towers and used to have a drawbridge. There is a parapet walkway right the way round.

Two buildings set at right angles to each other have windows with stone transoms and elegant moulding. There is a chapel in one of the towers at the entrance. It has ogival vaulting decorated with festoons and supported by colonettes in the purest of Flamboyant Gothic styles. A small chamber on the first floor was reserved for the castle owner.

Near the small church in **Saint-Pradoux-de-Mareuil** is Beauregard Castle built in the 14th Century. The main apartments are flanked by two towers and extend into a 17th-century wing in the form of a country house.

FROM TOP TO BOTTOM

Marouatte Castle is a vast residence which underwent major restoration during the 19th Century.

Vassaldie Castle.

The Château de Vendoire is a fine example of the great Classical-style mansions seen in the Mareuil area.

La Meyfrenie Castle in **Verteillac** dates from the 16th and 17th Centuries but it underwent alterations last century after damage by fire. The two projecting wings have disappeared, making the main façade more visible. The outbuildings surround a main courtyard and it is still possible to make out the wine cellars with their characteristic amenities and features.

La Vassaldie in **Gouts-Rossignol** was built on the top of a hill during the Classical Era. It has a main section topped by a rounded pediment, with a pavilion to either side roofed in the Mansart style. A balustrade runs right along the length of the façade. Two wings, set at right angles to the main apartments, line the courtyard which is closed off by a wide wrought-iron gate.

Another Classical mansion awaits us in **Vendoire**. The façades are decorated with carved pediments.

Connezac Castle, which was built over older remains, has two parts dating from the 17th and 18th Centuries and set at right angles to each other. There are pavilions to either side. A machicolated barbican borders what remains of the outer wall.

Bellussière House in **Rudeau-Ladosse** is an elegant 16th and 17th-century mansion with a fairly complex layout because it includes different architectural styles which the owners tried to combine in the 18th Century. It backs onto an old, splayed keep.

Les Combes used to be protected by a drawbridge across the moat. The right-angled buildings are flanked by towers on one side.

Standing at the top of a cliff is Aucors Castle in Beaussac. It is flanked by a polygonal tower and turrets with pepperpot roofs.

South of **Vieux-Mareuil**, halfway up the hill is Le Chanet, a 16th-century residence between a 15th-century crenelated tower and a corner lookout turret.

Let us stop our rush from one castle to the next and return to Périgueux, admiring, as we go, the old country residence of the Bishops of Périgueux, in **Château-l'Evêque**.

Tired with all this travelling, and our eyes dazzled with all that we have seen, let us now take time to eat, and discover the superb Périgord cuisine with a few friends. This is rustic cookery, full of subtleties and based on well-established traditions. Truffles and foie gras have pride of place but soup finished off with wine poured into the plate, pies of all kinds, stuffed poultry, golden-brown toast, penny bun mushrooms, fruit tarts and doughnuts, all washed down with generous quantities of wine from the Bergerac region, will give you a glimpse of the last, real face of Périgord – a face that shows you what good living is all about.

Index

Bibliography

AUDIERNE (A.), *Le Périgord illustré*, Périgueux, 1851.

AUDRERIE (D.), *Connaître les châteaux du Périgord*, Bordeaux, Éditions Sud Ouest, 1997.

BELINGARD (J.-M.), AUDRERIE (D.), CHAZAUD (E. DU), *Le Périgord des chartreuses*, Périgueux, Éditions Pilote 24, 2000.

Bulletins de la Société historique et archéologique du Périgord.

COCULA (A.-M.), *La Dordogne des bateliers*, Paris, Éditions Tallandier.

Étienne de La Boétie, Bordeaux, Éditions Sud Ouest, 1995.

Périgord, Bordeaux, Éditions Sud Ouest, 1999.

DELFAUD (P.), *Économie du département de la Dordogne*, Éditions Sud Ouest, Bordeaux, 2000.

DELLUC (B. et G.), ROUSSOT (A.), ROUSSOT-LARROQUE (J.), *Connaître la préhistoire en Périgord*, Bordeaux, Éditions Sud Ouest, 1991, rééd. 2001.

DESSALLES (L.), *Histoire du Périgord*, Périgueux, 1883-1886.

DUBOURG (J.), *Histoire des bastides d'Aquitaine*, Bordeaux, Éditions Sud Ouest, 1991.

DUBOURG (J.), *Connaître les bastides du Périgord*, Bordeaux, Éditions Sud Ouest, 1993.

ESCANDE (J.-J.), *Histoire du Périgord*, Cahors, 1934.

FAYOLLE (G.), *Histoire du Périgord*, Périgueux, Éditions Fanlac, 1983-1984.

FÉNELON (P.), *Périgord enchanté*, Artaud, Paris, 1966.

LACHAISE (B.) (séries under the direction of), *Histoire du Périgord*, Périgueux, Éditions Fanlac, 2000.

HIGOUNET-NADAL (H.) (séries under the direction of), *Histoire du Périgord*, Paris, Arthaud, 1966.

MICHEL (L.), *Le Périgord, le pays et les hommes*, Périgueux, Éditions Fanlac, 1969.

POMMARÈDE (P.), *Le Périgord oublié*, Périgueux, Éditions Fanlac, 1977.

ROCAL (G.), *Le Vieux Périgord*, Paris, 1927.

SECRET (J.), *L'Art en Périgord*, Dordogne Tourist Office, Périgueux, 1976.

VILLEPELET (R.), *La Formation du département de la Dordogne, étude de géographie politique*, Périgueux, 1908.

Carte Patrick Mérienne

Table of contents

Photographic credit

Dominique AUDRERIE: 88 top, 81 left. Alain BORDES: 14, 15 left, 16 right, 17, 19, 41 top left, 44 bottom, 62-63 top, 64, Bertrand CABROL: 34 top left, 76 bottom, 83 left, 84, 86, 89 left. Ray DELVERT: 30 left, 48, 49 top right, 49 bottom. Jean-Paul GISSEROT: 6 middle bottom, 9 middle bottom, 39, 51 right, 53 right, 54 top, 63 bottom, 73 right. J. B. LEROUX: 52. Pascal MOULIN: 2, 8, 9 middle top, 10 à 13, 16 right, 18 top and middle top, 19 à 27, 28 bottom, 29, 35 to 37, 38 left, 40 top, 46 right, 47, 49 top left, 50 middle top, 54 bottom, 55, 56, 59 à 61, 62 bottom, 66, 67, 69, 70, 74, 75, 76 top, 77 to 79, 84, 85, 87 bas, 91, 92 middle and bottom. Jean PLASSARD: 5. Philippe RALLION: 88 top. Guy-Marie RENIÉ: 3, 4, 6 bottom, 9 top and bottom, 15 right, 16 left, 18 middle and bottom, 28 top, middle and bottom, 30 right, 31, 32, 33, 34 top right, 38 right, 40 bottom, 41 bottom left, 41 right, 42-43, 44 except bottom, 45, 50, 51 left, 58, 71, 72, 73 left, 76 middle bottom, 80, 81 right, 82, 83 right, 87 top, 88 bottom, 89 right, 90, 92 top. Alain ROUSSOT: 53 top, 54 middle, 57 bottom. Richard ZÉBOULON: 65.

© Copyright 2001 – Editions Sud Ouest. Ce livre a été imprimé par Pollina à Luçon (85) – France.
La photogravure est de Photogravure d'Aquitaine à Bordeaux.
ISBN : 2.87901.416.6 – Editeur : 1080.01.05.03.01. – N° d'impression : L83217